Centerville Library
Washington-Centerville Public Library
DISCARD

Handbag
WORKSHOP

Design and Sew the Perfect Bag

By Anna Maia Mazur

Photography by Claire Benoist

The Taunton Press

Text and bag designs © 2014 by Anna Maia Mazur
Photographs © 2014 by Claire Benoist except where noted
Illustrations © 2014 by Christine Erikson
All rights reserved.

The Taunton Press
Inspiration for hands-on living®

The Taunton Press, Inc.
63 South Main Street
PO Box 5506
Newtown, CT 06470-5506
e-mail: tp@taunton.com

Executive Editor: Shawna Mullen
Assistant Editor: Tim Stobierski
Project Editor: Sarah Rutledge Gorman
Copy Editor: Candace B. Levy
Indexer: Barbara Mortenson
Cover and Interior Design: Stacy Wakefield Forte
Layout: Stacy Wakefield Forte
Illustrator: Christine Erikson
Photographer(s): Photos on pp. iv, 1, 4, 5, 8, 9, 14, 15, 21–26, 32, 36, 42, 54, 58, 64, 72, 78, 86–88, 96, 106, 116, 122, 132–134, 142, 150, 164 by Claire Benoist; all other photos by Anna Maia Mazur

The following names/manufacturers appearing in *Handbag Workshop* are trademarks: Big Bite™, Clover™, Craft-Fuse™, Crop-A-Dile™, Décor-Bond®, Fray Check™, Glad®, Glue Dots®, Hump Jumper®, Jo-Ann Stores℠, June Tailor®, Lowes℠, Lucite®, Microtex®, Newegg®, OLFA®, Pellon®, Peltex®, Press'n Seal®, Quarter Cut™, Scotch®, sewforless.com℠, ShirtTailor®, Snap Source®, SnapSetter®, Sulky®, Swarovski®, Tandy®, Teflon®, Tiffany®, Trex®, WAWAK®

Library of Congress Cataloging-in-Publication Data

Mazur, Anna M. (Ana Maia)
    Handbag workshop : design and sew the perfect bag / Anna M. Mazur.
        pages cm
    Summary: "This book presents 18 unique designer-lookalike handbags to sew, and teaches readers how to use favorite fabrics, leather, and faux leather to design and make the handbag of their dreams"-- Provided by publisher.
    Includes index.
    ISBN 978-1-62113-777-1 (paperback)
    1. Handbags. I. Title.
    TT667.M358 2014
    646.4'8--dc23
                          2014026519
Printed in the United States of America
10 9 8 7 6 5 4 3 2 1

NOTE: The templates in this book may be copied and enlarged for personal use only.

Dedication

I would like to dedicate this book to my husband, the love of my life; my wonderful children; and my parents, for their unconditional love and for instilling the values that made me who I am today. Pai, I can still picture your big smile, and if you were here you would be so proud.

Contents

INTRODUCTION

Bag making is in my blood. When I was about five years old, I made my first bag: a suitcase for my dolls. I crafted it from a sardine can—the type in which you insert a key at one end, then roll off the lid—which I thought resembled a soft-sided suitcase with a zipper that runs around three sides. I replaced the metal lid with a fabric cover in the same shape as the lid. I held the cover in place with a stick that I tied to the top of the can across the middle. This allowed me to lift the fabric lid on each end of the can so I could pack the "suitcase" (not that I could actually fit anything inside!).

What girl doesn't love bags? I, for one, can never have too many. A bag gives an outfit immediate polish and is the easiest way to add color to your wardrobe. Most of us have bags in an assortment of sizes and shapes, from practical to whimsical, just waiting to be filled with our daily essentials and tiny treasures. But sometimes you see, or already own, a bag that is not quite right—it's too bulky for daily use, or it can't hold enough, or it doesn't fit right under your arm. Or maybe you love its shape and size, but wish it were made out of another material.

A bag that is the correct size and the ideal shape, and created from quality leather or textile, sets a perfect mood. When you create a custom bag from a unique material, there will never be another one like it. This book shows you how to make the perfect bag customized to your particular needs. Chapter 1 lays out the basic framework needed to expand on simple geometric shapes and explains materials and supplies, while Chapter 2 reviews essential sewing techniques. Chapters 3 through 5 include eighteen original patterns that you can easily scale up or down to create your own perfect bags. The styles range from basic shapes—such as square, circle, triangle, and simple variations—to forms with an artistic flair.

Making a handbag is an investment of time and money. I strongly believe in durable, long-lasting materials and quality hardware. Most of the bags in this book are made out of genuine leather or a combination of leather and fabric. Seam allowances are $\frac{3}{8}$ inch for leather and $\frac{1}{2}$ inch for fabric. If you choose to use a leather pattern on fabric, simply increase the seam allowance, and vice versa. The patterns are designed to get you comfortable with the mechanics of making handbags and working with leathers so you can create truly one-of-a-kind gems.

What inspires a bag design? For me, a perfect leather, a to-die-for fabric, a magnificent color, a void in my collection, or just plain old need. The allure and aesthetic of a bag is not always about the label or who makes it, but rather a high-quality item crafted with fine materials and unexpected details. I design bags for function, and beauty follows. I think of a void and envision the ideal bag for a particular situation, then work backward to create it. Once I work out the design and finish a sample, I design the details and choose atypical materials for extra oomph.

When you begin to design a bag, the first decision is whether to re-create an existing concept or to develop your own. If you want to start fresh, think about the finished product and take it from there. Sketch out your thoughts so you can look back in chronological order. Don't expect your first draft to be your final idea. Having several thumbnails in front of you fosters creativity and allows you to tweak the concept until the perfect shape emerges. When you are drawing, make a checklist and ask yourself the following questions:

- What is the occasion?
- What size do I want?
- What aesthetics I am looking for—a streamlined bag or one with lots of details?
- How will I carry this bag?
- What strap style do I want?
- What will I make it out of?

Your answers will lead to additional questions, such as what you will use for the bag's foundation and support. Unless you're working with a tried-and-tested design, you'll have to experiment with various options to see what works and what doesn't.

Every handbag here is meticulously handcrafted with Old World charm. Each is unique in its own way. Enjoy!

HOW TO USE THIS BOOK

If you are just starting on your handbag-making journey and need an in-depth study, I recommend you read through the entire book in order, select a design from Chapter 3 (which features beginner bags), gather the necessary supplies (including the Basic Tool Kit, p. 12), and construct the bag. For those with more sewing experience and the necessary tools on hand, pick a bag, gather your supplies, and dive right in. In Chapter 2 you will find the basic sewing techniques that most projects will reference. For accuracy, make a full copy of pieces shown of fold.

CHAPTER ONE
BAG ANATOMY 101

The scope of handbag making is mind-boggling, but it doesn't have to be. You just need to understand the various bag shapes, know how a bag is put together, and have the proper tools and supplies on hand to get the job done. Once you are familiar with the basics, you will be able to analyze any style of bag and expand on and embellish it to suit your vision. The material your bag is made from can make or break its style. Many sewers are intimidated by working with leather, but it is actually very simple, and nearly every bag in this book is (or can be) made from leather. The thought of painting leather edges may be daunting, but it's a straightforward process when you are equipped with the right tools and have a comfortable, properly set up workspace. If you are just starting on your handbag-making journey, read through this chapter and the next one to gain an understanding of the basics and make sure you have a few essential tools. If you already

have experience and the necessary equipment, go ahead and pick a bag and start creating.

Handbag Shapes

Handbags come in all sorts of sizes and shapes. The permutations are endless, but they have one thing in common: They begin in the form of a simple geometric shape, usually a derivative of a rectangle, square, oval, or cylinder. When you manipulate this shape by slashing and spreading, then adding gussets and darts, the magic begins.

Understanding the Handbag Shape

In its simplest form, a handbag is just a box with up to six planes or surfaces, all of which have straight edges. There is a top, a front, a bottom, a back, and two sides.

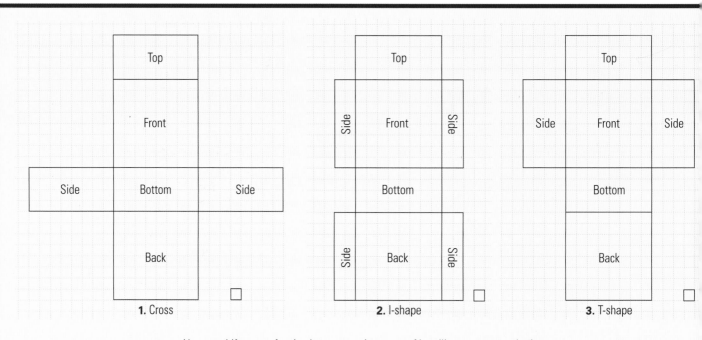

You can shift seams for simpler construction, ease of handling, or pure aesthetics.

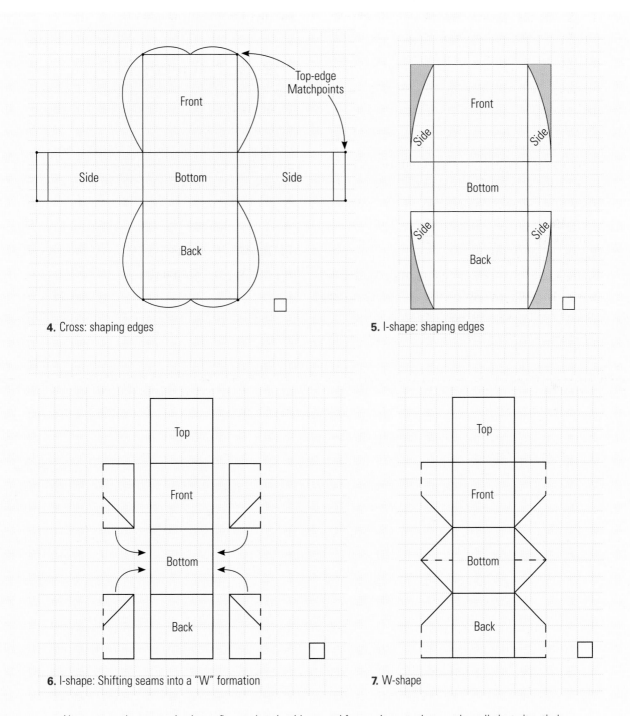

4. Cross: shaping edges

5. I-shape: shaping edges

6. I-shape: Shifting seams into a "W" formation

7. W-shape

You can turn the top section into a flap; replace it with a metal frame, zipper, or draw cord; or eliminate it entirely.

When you take from one plane and add to another, the cubic area does not change, as shown in the three distinct silhouettes on p. 6: a cross (1), the letter I (2), and a T shape (3). When folded, they are all the same size. You can design a multitude of bag shapes using these three simple grid formations. Think of these as possible slopers, or blueprints, for your bag.

Once you establish your framework, the next step is to alter it to your design specifications. When you manipulate the edges of one or more surfaces by adding, subtracting, or shaping, you transform the box into the unique design of your handbag (see p. 7). The next step is to execute a draft so you can see your creation in three dimensions. You can also draw on detailing, such as pocket placement and additional seams.

When designing a practical bag, keep in mind that you want a reinforced bottom, a secure top, an opening large enough for its contents, and pockets to keep everything organized. If you are always on the go and reaching for your bag, you will want handles that are long enough to throw over your shoulder, or one strap handle so you can carry the bag across your body.

Distinguishing Handbag Silhouettes

Handbag shapes tend to conform to tried-and-tested formulas, so many of the classics have not changed much over time; they have only been reimagined. Some style names are obvious indicators of the particular shape, whereas others come about by association. For example, in the 1950s Hermès redesigned a bag for Princess Grace Kelly, a trapezoid-shaped tote with a flap cover and a ridged top handle. That bag is now branded as the renowned Kelly Bag.

We associate five geometric shapes with certain bag styles: rectangle, square, oval, ellipse, and cylinder. Nearly every bag falls into one of these categories.

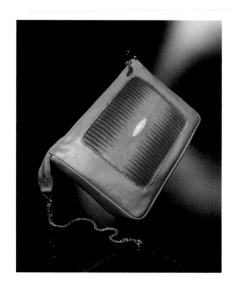

Rectangle or square

- **Backpack** A rectangle body and sides, carried in back, designed with two straps to be worn over the shoulders.
- **Baguette** An elongated rectangle body shaped with bottom corner darts and designed with one short strap in an east–west orientation; resembles a loaf of French bread (baguette).
- **Chanel** A flap-style bag featuring a topstitched quilting pattern.
- **Clutch** A strapless bag designed to be carried in the hand or under the arm.
- **Convertible** A rectangle you can hold in your hand or wear over your shoulder.
- **Cosmetic** A boxlike rectangle for storing toiletries.
- **Cross-body** A rectangle with a long strap; worn across the body.
- **Diaper** A boxlike bag for carrying baby necessities.
- **Doctor (Gladstone)** A roomy satchel-style bag toted by a doctor when making house calls; the opening is rigid to allow easy access to the contents.
- **Envelope** A slim bag with no depth.
- **Fanny/waist pack** A bag with a strap that buckles around the waist.
- **Flap** A rectangle body with a fold-over top and one strap in an east–west orientation.
- **Fold-over** A bag that folds down on itself.

- **Frame** A bag with a ridge opening.
- **Kelly** A ladylike satchel-style bag.
- **Messenger** A sturdy bag for lugging around documents; it has a long strap and is carried across the body.
- **Minaudière** A small decorative evening bag held in the hand and usually adorned with jewels and semi-precious stones.
- **Satchel** A structured bag with a rectangular bottom and two short handles.
- **Shopper** A medium-size bag with a large top opening and short or long handle straps.
- **Shoulder** A bag with one or two long straps designed to be carried on one shoulder.
- **Tote** A large bag with a wide top opening with short handle straps; used to transport groceries, books, and other items.
- **Train case** A roomy barrel-shaped bag that can carry overnight essentials or paperwork.
- **Weekender** A large bag with short handles used for transporting provisions for a weekend getaway; may have wheels.
- **Wristlet** A small bag with a braceletlike carrying strap that slides easily over the hand.

- **Hobo** A soft bag with one handle that hangs from the shoulder; it has a crescentlike opening and a zippered top.
- **Saddle** A shape that connects two bags with a strap; designed to be draped over a horse's back.
- **Sphere** A bag shaped like a globe.
- **Toaster** Similar to a bowler bag but more angular.

Cylinder

- **Barrel** A rectangle body with rounded sides.
- **Bowler** A dome-shaped body with squished oval sides and two short handles.
- **Bucket** A rectangle body with a rounded bottom and hand or shoulder straps.
- **Drawstring** A rectangle body with a gathered top edge and a bottom in a round, oval, rectangle, or square shape.
- **Duffle** An oversize barrel used for traveling or carrying sports equipment.
- **Sling** A backpack with only one strap.

Oval or ellipse

- **Bowler** Originally made for carrying a bowling ball.
- **Crescent** A bag with a semicircular shape and/or opening.

Soft-Sided Versus Hard-Sided Bags

Soft-sided bags are versatile, go-anywhere carryalls that have a playful ease, whereas hard-sided bags are structured and dramatic but also more difficult to put together.

Soft bags

Soft bags evoke a sense of a free spirit and laid-back glamour. The foremost shape is the hobo. Soft bags are much easier than hard bags for the average sewing machine to handle, and sewers of all ages and skills enjoy creating soft bags. Most start with a basic tote shape made from a simple cotton or home-decorating fabric. These types of bags aren't terrifically sturdy, so for a long-term option and an instant style upgrade, employ soft or imitation leather.

Hard bags

The classic hard-sided bag has timeless appeal. Its beauty lies in its minimalism and sophisticated, subtle details. Hard bags are more of a challenge to make, but they are by no means impossible. Traditionally they require highly specialized sewing machines, such as the ones used by cobblers. These machines can pierce through incredible thicknesses and have virtually no sewing beds that get in the way, so you can get into very tight spaces. For a home sewer without access to this type of equipment, you'll have to get creative. Folds will need to be scored. Prepiercing the sewing holes makes for stress-free hand stitching. Piercing pliers are available, and they come with one or more prongs; the multiprong style allows you to pierce evenly spaced holes without any marking. The end prong is inserted into the last hole pierced. To stitch a strong seamline, use two needles and a shoelike lacing technique.

Sewing with Leather Versus Cloth

The first step to sewing with leather (real or faux) is to find a lightweight or garment-weight leather that you absolutely love, then buy a sample swatch. Sew a simple seam to check how your machine handles it under the presser foot. Does the leather feed smoothly under the presser foot? If not, you may wish to try a Teflon® foot. Check that the needle style and size is suitable for your leather and adjust as needed. Keep an eye on the tension and stitch length and make sure the thread is the correct strength. Once you know your machine will sew a leather seam, the next step is to test out the topstitching capabilities. Pound the seam open, and from the top, edgestitch on each side of the seam (see p. 111, Step 8). After you have confirmed your machine can handle the leather you have selected, go ahead and purchase enough for the pattern.

Painting Edges

Setting up your space for painting leather edges is all about comfort, good lighting, suitable paint, and the right tools. Painting edges is not a difficult task; it just takes patience. The more relaxed you are, the more precise you will be. Good task lighting and a table with a comfortable working height are indispensable. After trying an assortment of artist paintbrushes, toothpicks, and craft sticks, I found that a stainless-steel edge paddle works best. The paint sticks to the paddle, but it also releases easily. The paddle has differently shaped tip ends that are perfect for picking up various amounts of paint. The square end lets you apply paint to a precise point, whereas the rounded end works well on broader area. The paint is permanent when it dries, but you do have a few moments to wipe off mistakes. Always keep a damp rag nearby. As soon as any excess paint seeps over the edge, clean it with a quick light brushing motion, using a delicate swipe with a simple turn of the wrist and a fast dab. Wipe from the bag segment out to and off the edge.

Cover the work surface with an absorbent layer of paper towels or terry cloth so unintentional drips are soaked up immediately and before you accidentally move your work across the wet paint. Prevent spills by placing the paint bottle inside a larger container so the paint will be confined if it tips over. I find that for most small paint bottles, a pint or quart plastic container from the deli works especially well. This is large enough to contain a spill and yet small enough to prevent the bottle from tipping over all the way.

Essential Supplies

If you are new to sewing and patternmaking, you will need a specific set of tools, some of which may be unfamiliar to you. I highly recommend gathering these items *before* you dive into any of the projects. As with all sewing projects, you will need sharp scissors, a rotary cutter and mat, marking pens and pencils, see-through rulers, a French curve, a steel-edge ruler with cork back, a clear grid ruler with metal cutting edge, a utility knife, pattern paper, straight pins, and plenty of small binder clips for nonpinnable materials. But there is also a whole host of additional specialized tools that will smooth the way for you.

Needle and thread

Bag seams have to be sturdy because they will hold up the bag contents. Ordinary garment-weight cotton-covered polyester is sufficient for most cloth seams, but for leather seams you will need a sturdier thread in upholstery or topstitching weight. (My machine dislikes heavyweight threads, so I double up the needle thread, which produces a very sturdy seam.) You will need a selection of machine needles in various sizes and types. Unlike in a garment, the seam thickness within the same handbag can vary drastically. For example, a size 12 needle will easily sew two pieces of leather together, but when those pieces are folded at the seam to become an edge, the two layers become four. Topstitching through four layers may now require a size 18 needle. Stitch length is also important in both fabric and leather; the heavier and thicker the fabric or leather, the longer the stitch length.

Cutting and pressing surfaces

You can cut leather with an ordinary pair of scissors, but a metal-edge ruler and rotary cutter will produce the straightest cut edges. As a result, your seams—especially those with exposed edges—will be straighter and have a dye-cut edge. My go-to cutting surface is a rigid self-healing plastic mat. It's worth every penny to invest in a good cutting mat. This will improve your cutting efficiency, prolong the life of your blades, and last for years (so it will eventually pay for itself—mine is more than 15 years old and still in good shape). Ideally, you want a fairly large mat that covers an entire table so you can fit all the bag pieces on the cutting surface. When you are cutting stiff leathers, you will likely use a utility knife instead of a rotary cutter. On these occasions, feel free to use a less expensive mat.

An iron and a traditional ironing board are fine for cloth, but leather seams need to be pressed with a mallet over a smooth, hard surface, such as granite. Don't be tempted to press your seams on your kitchen counter; instead, buy a small slab available from a leather source or a granite supplier. Granite is heavy, so stick to a 12-inch to 18-inch square. (The piece left over from cutting out a sink is a good size and not too heavy to lift.) Mallets come in rubber and plastic and in various weights. Depending on the leather weight, you will want to have a couple of different types of mallets on hand. You also need a seam stick, a ham, and a point presser so you can open straight and curved seams without leaving an impression of the seam allowance. The gadgets you are pressing over need to be sturdy enough to take the pounding. A regular seam stick, although made of hardwood, is too soft. Ipé wood and Trex® siding (use the smooth side) are firm enough, and they work well when cut into small pieces and narrow strips. A mini cast-iron anvil has various angles that you can use as pressing

BASIC TOOL KIT

- Adhesives, including adhesive dot roller, all-purpose white glue, leathercraft cement, contact adhesive spray, temporary spray adhesive like Sulky®, rubber cement, double-face tape (⅛-, ¼-, and ⅜-inch), easy-release tape, and blue painters' tape
- Card stock for drafting patterns
- Cutting tools, including rotary cutter, utility knife, serrated knife, awl, edge beveler, skiver, hand-sewing leather punch, Crop-A-Dile™ II Big Bite™ punch, hole punches, and self-healing plastic cutting mat
- Foundations, interfacing, and bag stiffener
- French curves and circle templates
- Gift-wrapping tissue paper
- Hard surface, such as mini anvil or granite slab
- Hardware, such as screwdriver, hammer, vise, and fine-tooth saw

- Latex or plastic gloves
- Lighter for singeing cord/zipper ends
- Marking tools, including pencils, chalk marker, fabric marking pens, and erasable markers
- Needles for hand sewing and machine sewing, Hump Jumper® attachment for stitching over thick fabric humps, thimble, and glover's or leather hand-sewing needles
- Painting tools, including soft-tip paintbrush, stiff-tip paintbrush, paint sponges, and stainless-steel edge paddle
- Paints, dyes, and stains
- Pattern paper or butcher's paper
- Pins, small office binder clips, curved hair clips, Glad® Press'n Seal®, and Fray Check™ for sealing seams
- Pliers such as needle-nose, round-nose, side-cutting, and crimping
- Pressing tools: iron, seam stick, ham, and point presser

- Rivet setter, and rivets in an assortment of sizes and colors
- Rubber mallet for working leather into shape
- Rulers, including see-through ruler, protractor, slotted ruler (such as June Tailor® Quarter Cut™), steel-edge ruler with cork back, and clear grid ruler with metal cutting edge
- Sandpaper
- Scissors, including pinking and scalloping shears
- Sewing thread
- Teflon feet and other specialty feet for your sewing machine, such as zipper foot
- Thread including all-purpose, button, top-stitching, carpet, and embroidery floss
- Tweezers
- Zipper yardage with white tape and zipper sliders

surfaces, and rocks are like miniature hams that you can insert into tight spots. Next time you are outside, gather a few rocks in several sizes and shapes, wash them well, and add them to your pressing inventory.

Foundations and interfacing

A bag is made up of one or more layers: the exterior, (the facade), and the interior (or lining). Between the two layers is the inner structure, called the foundation or interlining. This unseen layer is often more important than the outside of the bag. Strategically placed hidden panels can provide additional foundation support. A bag with the proper inner structure will have built-in control and shape retention that ensures stability. It will hold up the contents, wear well, and last for years. It is important to think about how the bag will be used, how much weight will it carry, and how it will be cleaned. A bag for daily use needs a good foundation and, most important, a sturdy base that will not tear. A bag that will be washed obviously needs to be made from a sturdy fabric, while a bag that can only be spot cleaned requires a water-repellent coating.

Depending on the bag size, style, and material, you can use a variety of foundations for support, from sew-in to fusible interfacings to self-fabric. For leathers and heat-sensitive fabrics, choose a sew-in; for all others, fusibles are wonderful. When selecting a foundation, keep in mind it will add bulk within the seam allowances, but there are ways to get around this. I call it a foundation sandwich. To make the sandwich, simply cut the foundation without the seam allowances and add to it a lightweight layer that is cut the same size as the bag. Secure the foundation to the layer by sewing all around the foundation edge. Treat the foundation sandwich like an interlining. The following lists include various types of materials that can be used to strengthen a bag or support the bottom.

Lining

You will need to have several types of linings on hand: a stiffener for bag bases, sew-in and iron-on interfacing, foam sheeting, and buckram.

- **Bag stiffener** This cardboardlike product reinforces the base of the bag bottom and hardware; it cuts easily with scissors and is washable.
- **Buckram** Stiff cloth made of cotton or linen.
- **Fleece** Best for soft linings—easy to handle and easy to sew.
- **Flexible chopping mat** Ideal for adding structure to soft-sided bags; it cuts easily with scissors.
- **Foam sheets** Thin craft foam makes a nice cushion to protect your electronic devices.
- **Iron-on interfacings** Stabilize and beef up weak fabric.

- **Pellon® Craft-Fuse™** Used to provide light- to medium-weight stabilization.
- **Pellon Décor-Bond®** Used to provide firm stabilization.
- **Pellon Peltex®** Ultra-firm stabilizing fabric.
- **ShirtTailor®** Finely woven cotton shirting fabric.

Adhesives

Adhesives are your ally in the handbag-making arena. But a word of caution: A little goes a long way. Whenever you work with any type of glue, it is a good idea to have a damp cloth available to wipe off excess from your hands and tools. Cover your work surface with plastic when working with an adhesive and place the glue and a damp towel in dishpans so if the glue spills, it is contained and a towel is always within reach.

Whenever you are selecting a type of adhesive, keep in mind the end purpose. Do you require stiff holding power or do you need the fabric to stay flexible? If you are affixing a base to the bottom support, you will probably need glue with holding power, like a contact cement. On the other hand, if you are gluing down a leather seam allowance, you will want it to stay flexible, so select your product accordingly.

There are so many adhesives on the market that you can probably find a different glue for every project, but you need only a few types. I like a liquid in cement and rubber form that is odorless, cleans up quickly with water, and spreads easily. You also need a decent time frame between applying the glue and bringing the sections together, and aerosols are handy for covering large areas. Double-face tape in a narrow width provides great holding power. It is flexible, like rubber cement, but without the gooeyness, so you have ultimate control. It functions much like pins in sewing. The drawback is that it will gum up your needle, so be sure to place it strategically.

CHAPTER TWO
SEWING TECHNIQUES

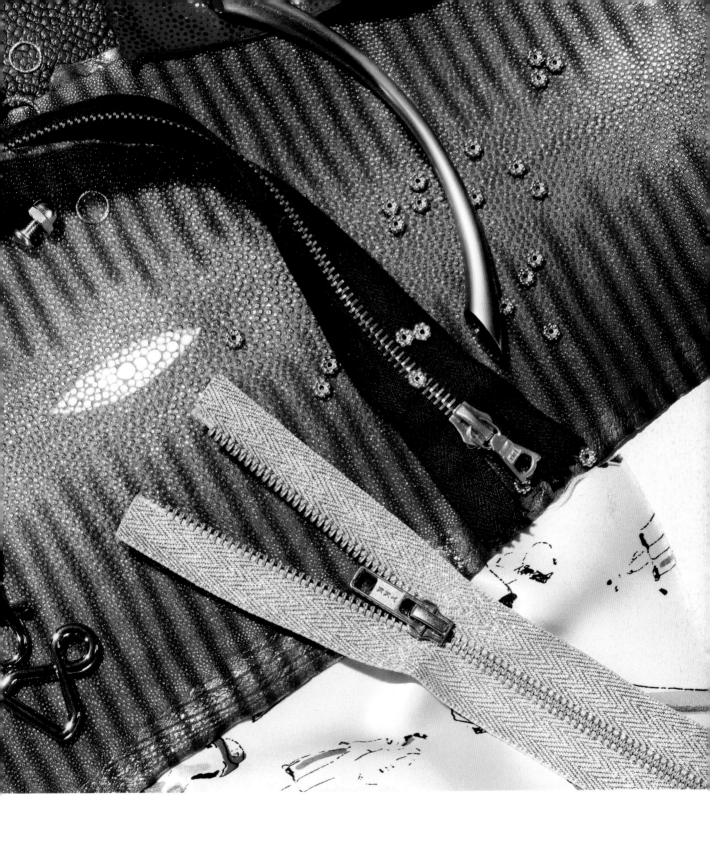

Pictured is the base of a bag ready to be pressed, along with tools for pressing leather seams that replace your ironing board and iron.

In this chapter you will learn the fundamental sewing techniques for putting a bag together. The best and easiest way to get comfortable with any of the projects in this book is to practice by creating little samples, especially if you are new to handbag making. These experiments are also more fun than merely jotting down notes, and they act as a physical reminder of what works—and what doesn't. You can also get great new ideas from your samples.

Making a bag differs from creating a garment in several aspects. You are dealing with shorter and narrower seams that, in many instances, you have to coax under your presser foot. Most seam errors on leather, unfortunately, cannot be undone, but simply sewing at a slower speed helps prevent many mistakes. Keep in mind that within the same bag you will be switching needle types and/or sizes as well as presser foot styles, which is another reason to avoid rushing. A well-made design has perfectly executed stitching lines with no overlapped stitches, no visible thread tails, and raw edges that are dressed with a coating. Painting leather edges is a straightforward process when you are equipped with the right tools and have a comfortable workspace that is properly set up. Decorative stitching looks nice when done with a heavier thread, ideally for topstitching. If you can't find the right color of topstitching thread, or your machine can't handle the heavier weight, use two threads in the needle. This trick also allows you to customize your color by blending two shades.

Rivets, when set properly, are as secure as a sewn seam. Hole punchers are handy for precutting holes for hand sewing as well as for rivets and eyelets. It's worth investing in a hand-sewing leather punch and a Crop-A-Dile II Big Bite punch. One cuts holes for needles up to $3/32$ inch, while the other has a 6-inch neck clearance that is perfect for cutting areas that are farther in from an edge. It not only cuts the $1/8$-inch holes for the rivets that are used throughout this book, but it also punches $3/16$-inch holes and sets snaps and eyelets without creating hand fatigue. Both tools are great investments and you will use them in so many other applications beyond making handbags.

Sewing Basics

Assembling a handbag opens up opportunities for using sewing techniques not necessarily required elsewhere. Seams are usually pounded with a mallet and then glued, riveted, or bolted together. You can leave exposed edges in their natural state or treat them with dyes and paints. When your layers are too thick for the machine, you can use a wide array of tools to pierce sewing holes.

Seams

Seams are a critical element of any handbag. They do not just hold the bag together but must also be robust enough to handle the weight of the bag's contents. I generally use $3/8$-inch seam allowances on leather and $1/2$ inch on fabric. For additional strength, stitch with two threads through the needle or use a heavier thread. For thicker layers, increase the stitch length. Exposed seams are a mainstay of a bag. You can choose from many products to coat the edges, from paints to dyes to gum tragacanth, a clear, gumlike substance that binds the fuzzy fibers and stiffens the edge slightly. It is meant for slicking and burnishing edges on vegetable-tanned leather, but you can also use it on leathers that are chrome tanned.

Neat stitching lines are important. A well-made bag has no overlapped stitching, and all thread tails are concealed. An easy fix is to pull all the tails to the wrong side, then tie them. When you need to break up a line of stitching, simply start stitching at the last sewn hole. Once the threads are pulled to the wrong side, the line will look uninterrupted. Tied thread tails look messy, especially if they will be seen. After tying, thread them on a needle (an embroidery needle with a large eye makes threading several strands painless) and insert the needle at the base of the knot. Push the needle between the layers, $1/2$ inch or so, and bring it back out. If you pull on the thread, the knot will bury itself. Then simply trim the tails flush with the bag. With leather, take an extra precaution: You don't want to create additional holes, so insert the needle into an existing hole, traveling between the leather layers and exiting at another preexisting hole. If there is only one skin layer, move the needle within the skin.

Even after all these years at the sewing table, I still test out seams. This allows me to choose the right combination of needle plus thread color and weight, and also helps me determine the most appropriate seam type to best showcase the specific material on hand. The testing also clues me in on how the built-up layers will look; what seam finish is needed; how best to treat the exposed edges; and how the fiber reacts to heat, steam, and pressing. If you work out all these issues before delving into a project, you are guaranteed a successful outcome.

On fabric bags you can use traditional garment seams, which are pressed as sewn to set the stitches and then pressed open. Leather requires a different approach, and you can use several seaming techniques, from standard to overlapped to butted, by which a strip is placed underneath and edgestitched in place. I prefer to sew a traditional seam on leather with a $3/8$-inch seam allowance. This narrower seam cuts down on trimming and, obviously, requires less leather. (It is amazing how much you save by simply reducing the seam allowance from ⅝ inch to ⅜ inch.) Next, I use a rubber mallet to pound the seam open and then, from the right side, edgestitch on each side close to the seamline through all layers. Another strategy is to tape down the seam allowances with flexible double-face tape, which works like rubber cement. When machine stitching in tight and problematic areas, for the most accuracy it is best to hand-walk the line of stitching. Switch between styles of presser feet. The zipper foot can come in handy in these areas.

A one- or two-piece bag is simple enough to construct, but when the design involves multiple pieces construction becomes more involved. All the sections play a role, and each piece needs to fit snugly against another, much like a jigsaw puzzle. Cutting accuracy is critical. If the pieces are not cut to their proper dimensions, the assembly will be more difficult. It is equally important to make sure your seam allowance is accurate, and be sure to transfer all match points.

One of the more difficult tasks in bag making is sewing around sharp corners, where inside and outside edges meet. This is generally not a problem in traditional garment sewing, as the concave edge is stabilized, clipped, and spread open to meet the convex edge. But with a handbag, clipping into the seam allowances can weaken the seamline and potentially deteriorate the corners, the very place where the bag will take a beating. To ease the process of going around sharp corners, I use a partial arc from a 2-inch circle to round them off slightly.

Leather

When sewing with leather, a rubber mallet and a hard surface are the replacement for your iron and ironing board (see p. 16). Sewing a bag from leather is very rewarding from a cost standpoint because markup in stores is so substantial, and in some ways the process is much easier than sewing from cloth. Leather does not ravel, so you can get away with narrower seam allowances, which are much easier to handle and drastically reduce trimming time. Seams on tissue-weight leathers need to be stabilized with strips of fusible interfacing. Using a cool iron and a pressing cloth to protect the leather, lightly fuse ½-inch strips of interfacing to all the seam allowances, aligning the long edges on the interfacing strip with the leather's cut edge. For curved edges, slash the interfacing at ½-inch intervals, from one edge to the other, but do not cut through; leave a hinge. In convex areas, align the hinge on the interfacing strip with the leather's cut edge and overlap the slashes over the seam allowance. In concave areas, place the hinge just beyond the seamline and overlap the slashes over the seam allowance.

NOTE You cannot pin leather layers together for sewing because the pins will create permanent holes. Instead, use small office binder clips to temporarily hold the layers.

Traditional presser feet will stick to leather, so use a Teflon foot, which will usually allow the seams to feed smoothly. In cases when even a Teflon foot will stick, such as when sewing on the right side of patent leather, cover the stitching area with strips of sealable plastic wrap, like Glad Press'n Seal. The plastic will help the presser foot glide effortlessly over the leather. After stitching, it tears off easily and leaves no residue.

When sewing with leather, be sure to select a needle that is heavy enough and has a very sharp tip. Sometimes a traditional leather needle is not ideal because it pierces the material with little slashed lines and creates a weaker seam. I prefer to use a Microtex® needle in the weight appropriate for the project. The point is very sharp and pierces the leather with a fine round hole. You can use traditional sewing machine thread in the needle and bobbin, but for extra strength double up and use two strands through the needle. A longer-than-normal stitch length makes for a stronger seam, so use 8 stitches per inch instead of 12. Don't backstitch or overlap the stitching—overpiercing the leather weakens the seam. Begin and end your stitches in the same hole, pull all threads to the wrong side, tie together in a square knot, and trim the tails ¼ inch away from the knot.

To press open leather seams, place the material on a granite slab and use a rubber mallet to pound the seams open. There are several ways to keep them open. My preferred method is to edgestitch through all layers from the right side on either side of the seam. You can also glue down the seam allowances with leathercraft cement or use double-face tape.

Straps

Straps are the backbone of a handbag. They are often the first element I think about when I begin to design. I ask myself if I will carry the bag over my shoulder, across my body, in the crook of my arm, or in my hand. I consider how sturdy and resilient the handles need to be, whether there will be one or two straps, if they will be made from the same fabric as the bag, whether they will be structured or soft, and if they will incorporate a chain or other hardware.

Your design decisions will influence how and where the straps attach to the bag. Strap styles vary greatly. They can be part of the bag body, as in a hobo style, or made separately out of self-fabric, leather, Lucite®, bangles, beaded strands, simple utilitarian nylon webbing, or basic chains in everything from ordinary metals to more ornate and precious ones. Strap lengths can vary widely, and they can be adjustable. They can attach side to side, as in an east–west formation, or you can have double straps with one attached to the front and one to the back. Be sure to consider comfort when deciding on a strap style. For example, a metal chain can be a beautiful choice, but it's neither comfortable nor practical to use on a bag that will hang from your shoulder all day. I like to create at least two strap choices for every handbag so that I have the option of carrying the bag in several ways. I integrate the first strap into the design, and I like to make the second one

HOW TO MAKE A BASIC 1-INCH FACED LEATHER STRAP

Cut two strips of leather in 2-inch and 1-inch widths to the desired length. Set aside the 1-inch strip, which will become the facing. Working on the wrong side of the 2-inch strip, lightly brush with leathercraft cement. Wait a few minutes, until the cement becomes cloudy and tacky. Fold both long edges so they meet at center. Press firmly. Place the strap on a hard surface (granite works best) and pound the edges to thin them out. Next, add the facing to the strap. Spread the cement on the backs of the facing strip and strap. After it becomes cloudy and tacky, align the long edges and press the strips together. Let the glue settle and dry, then topstitch the strap with parallel rows of stitching.

inconspicuous (and usually detachable). For example, the "Fold-Over Frame Bag" (p. 42) includes a clever inner pocket designed to neatly hide the permanently attached chain strap so it does not hang loose inside the bag and get tangled with all the contents.

Linings

Linings run the gamut from simple to luxurious, and they can provide hidden glamour. I think a bag should look just as nice on the inside as on the outside. In a bag with a top closure, only you know a delectable lining is inside, and once in a while someone else catches a glimpse of your secret treasure. In addition to its beauty, a lining adds resilience. It is one of the most important elements of the inner structure because it supports the handbag's contents and bears the brunt of the weight. An ideal lining is made from a feather-weight fabric that is light enough to keep the bag weight to a minimum but sufficiently sturdy to withstand wear and tear.

Within the lining walls you can get creative with custom-size pockets specifically tailored to your needs. Think of the lining as a blank canvas, and take the opportunity to use unexpected materials, like ponte knits, suede, silk, and floral prints. Just remember to stabilize stretchy fabrics with interfacing and to stay away from fabrics that are rough to the touch or snag easily. Linings do not normally require much fabric, so it is a great way to use leftovers, especially sentimental scraps. If you don't have enough for the entire lining, just add a touch. For example, making a zippered pocket from a treasured fabric will cause you to smile every time you see it. The decision of whether to use a drop-in or an integrated lining usually depends on the bag's style. An integrated lining is added to the bag while it is sewn, whereas a drop-in lining is finished separately and added to the bag in the final stage, usually attached to the top edge or to the edge of the facing.

When you come across the perfect lining but discover it is not compatible with your project, all hope is not lost: You can fuse any yardage with iron-on interfacing, then cut out the lining as needed. For example, the lining of the "Stingray Zip-Top Wristlet Clutch" (p. 78) is made from a beautiful charmeuse print that reminds me of the Roaring Twenties, *The Great Gatsby*, and old-time movies—perfect for this bag. But the fabric was too light to use on its own, so I used Craft-Fuse to strengthen it. Be sure to fuse before cutting. Both the fabric and the interfacing can shrink during the fusing process, so if you cut out the lining and interfacing separately and then fuse them together, chances are the pieces will shrink and no longer fit the bag.

HIDING POCKETS

Functional pockets are not just for the interior. You can hide them on the outside between the seam allowances using an invisible zipper for the closure, within a slot-like opening, under a welt, or behind a zippered window. Use function to determine where and how to place an external pocket. For example, a slot opening is unobtrusive and can keep your mobile phone easily accessible. Keys always seem to fall into an abyss, so they also deserve their own exterior pocket.

Pockets

These days we all take for granted that most bags will have a minimum of three pockets in the lining—mobile phone, patch, and zippered—but this was not always the case. Years ago I spent weeks hunting for a diaper bag with individual compartments that would hold everything in an organized fashion. That's when I created my first customized insert. From the outside it looked like a plain leather tote bag, but on the inside everything was methodically arranged like a mini file cabinet. Adding the insert to the finished bag was more work than if I had started from scratch. From that point forward, I planned ahead for the pockets I would need and made sure I incorporated them into the design.

NOTE Pockets are made from simple squares and rectangles. The easiest way to cut them is to simply tear the fabric so the pockets will always be on grain.

The number of pockets relates directly to the size of the handbag. The bigger the bag, the more surface area available for fastening pockets. Lifestyle also dictates the need for pockets. For example, an urban dweller who walks frequently would likely appreciate holsters for a water bottle and an umbrella in a workday bag. Keep in mind that the more pockets you have, the more you stress the bag's lining. To minimize wear and tear, stabilize the lining—or, ideally, interface it entirely. At a minimum, the pocket stress points need to be reinforced. You can also opt for a heavier lining, but it will weigh down the bag. No matter how small the bag is, I always add the three basic pockets, as well as a pen slot and pocket for a small notepad. (Leaving home without my pen and pad is like departing without my keys.)

Zippers

Prepackaged zippers generally come in predetermined lengths, limited colors, and only a handful of weights. The zipper's tooth size is generally engraved on the back of the slider; the higher the number, the larger the zipper. When you don't have the right color or you can't find the right length, turn to zipper by the yard. Once you try it, you will never go back to the prepackaged kind. You can cut zipper by the yard into any length and custom dye the white tapes. You will need two essential tools: side-cutting pliers to remove a small section of teeth or coil to make it easy to insert the slider, and a utility lighter to sear the cut edges so they don't ravel. You generally do not need stops, as the zipper ends will be enclosed within a seam. If there is a chance the slider could slide off, add a small rivet. If the zipper tail is freestanding, cover it with a pull tab. You can also experiment with the number of sliders, as those with plastic coils can zip smoothly in either direction. This means you can add more than one slider and make a double-ended zipper. Two pulls can zip to the center, or they can begin at the center and zip to the sides. Metal teeth zip smoothly in only one direction (unless you use a 2-way slider), but you can insert two sliders to meet at the center (one slider will just not slide as smoothly as the other).

You can customize zipper by the yard by buying all the components separately, including the zipper tape,

A #5 metal tooth zipper.

the sliders, and the pulls. When you begin with a zipper with white tape, you can dye it, paint it, embroider it, or embellish it with beads and rhinestones. Teeth come in different weights and styles, from metal to coil to molded plastic to rhinestone, and they are available in nearly every imaginable color and finish. You can further customize a zipper by decorating the slider with a tassel or ready-made pull, and some sliders are available with an open hook. With this type of slider, you can custom build a fancy pull out of components, such as jewelry findings. Simply create the decorative embellishment, insert it into the open hook, and use pliers to close it up.

THE BAGS

CHAPTER THREE

BEGINNER BAGS

CHAPTER FOUR
INTERMEDIATE BAGS

CHAPTER FIVE
ADVANCED BAGS

BEGINNER BAGS

T HE BAGS IN THIS CHAPTER have straightforward shapes, but they are far from boring. Simple designs often have the greatest impact and make a lasting impression. Exceptional material, quality hardware, smooth topstitching, and thin, crisp edges are hallmarks of a well-made bag. The sewing is uncomplicated, but it can get tricky depending on your fiber selection. The key to success is knowing how your machine will handle leather seams, then sorting out what you will sew by machine and what you will do by hand. You also need to know what types of glues are best suited for your project and when and where to use them, how to shift seams from problematic areas to where they can be easily sewn, techniques for separating zippers for ease of installation, ways to prevent seams from jamming under the presser foot, how to eliminate bulky edges, and techniques for smooth topstitching.

Dimensions: 9½ inches wide by
6½ inches high

Seam allowance: ⅜ inch,
unless otherwise noted

Fibers: Lamb suede and metallic organza

BEGINNER

Security Pouch

TOOLS AND MATERIALS

Basic Tool Kit (p. 12)

10-inch by 13-inch lamb suede

10-inch by 13-inch metallic organza
for lining

Size 10 Microtex needle

10 inches of zipper tape,
#3 metal teeth

#3 zipper slider

Swivel clasp

Five ⅜-inch solid metal rings

Three ⅝-inch solid metal rings

Heavy-duty jump ring

Figure-eight connector

TEMPLATES

Wrist strap and two anchors,
cut one, 1⅛ inch by 18½ inch,
(in suede)

Rectangles, cut two,
10 inch by 13 inch (one in suede and
one in lining fabric)

YOU CAN CARRY this sweet little bag on its own or safely tucked away inside a bigger one (see "Fur-Lined Mini Shopper," p. 150). When the strap is attached to the ring on the other end of the strap or to the set attached to the zipper slider, it's a wristlet. You can hang it over your arm when the strap is hooked to the ring on the anchor attached to the opposite side of the bag. If you attach an optional long strap (see p. 163) to the rings on the edges, it becomes a shoulder bag. The version pictured is made from velvety suede and lined in a crisp metallic organza.

Prepare the zipper

1. The teeth on a metal zipper have little knobs that lock together, and these must be oriented in the same direction for the zipper to work. Although you can insert a slider from either end, it will zip smoothly only if the knobs face away from the slider (1a). To make it easier to insert the slider, use side-cutting pliers to snip about five teeth at each end so you have about ⅜ inch of exposed zipper tape. Do this on all four edges (1b). Use a utility lighter to carefully sear the cut edges (1c).

Make and insert the pouch

2. On the right side of the bag, place one section of the zipper tape along one edge and the other section on the opposite edge, keeping the raw edge even with the zipper tape edge (see 2a). Stitch ¼ inch from the raw edge. This is the middle of the zipper tape, and there is a distinct line in the weave that you can follow as a guide (2a). Place the lining on the top of the bag and pin it along the zipper edges. Sew over the previous stitching (2b). If the lining is not see-through, flip the bag over and sew from the other side where you can see the stitching. Turn the bag right side out through one of the sides. From the right side, topstitch through all layers, ¼ inch away from the fold. Repeat on other edge (2c).

3. On the long edge, machine-baste the lining to the bag ¼ inch away from the raw edge. Repeat on the other long edge (3a). Insert the zipper slider, paying careful attention to the direction to ensure it zips smoothly (3b; see 1a). Close both ends of the zipper tape, hand-stitching the edges together while keeping the back of the bag free (3c).

Make the strap

4. Fold the strap piece lengthwise into thirds and stitch close to the long edge. Some edges just don't want to stay together, so fold as you go. For an unobstructed view in front of the presser foot, use tweezers for extra precision (4a). Come up on the other side of the strip and topstitch close to the fold (4b).

5. Cut the strap into three pieces: one 14-inch piece for the wrist strap (which includes a ¾-inch turn-under on each end) and two 2¼-inch pieces for the strap anchors. Attach the swivel clasp to one end of the wrist strap, threading the strap through the eye of the clasp and turning back ¾ inch. Hand-stitch the end to secure (5a). Thread a small metal ring through the strap and sew it over the seam to conceal the joint (5b). On the other end of the wrist strap, insert a small metal ring (which will be used to conceal the joint) and a large metal ring. Turn back ¾ inch over the large ring and hand-stitch.

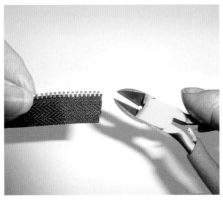

1a. Metal teeth orientation: knobs facing away from slider. 1b. Snip teeth. 1c. Sear edges.

2a. Stitch ¼ inch from raw edge.

2b. Sew lining.

2c. Topstitch through all layers.

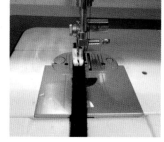

3a. Machine-baste lining on long edge.

3b. Insert zipper slider.
3c. Hand-stitch edges.

4a. Hold folded edges with tweezers.
4b. Topstitch close to fold.

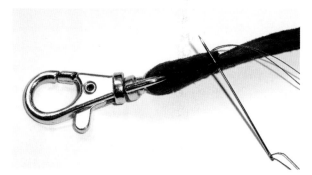

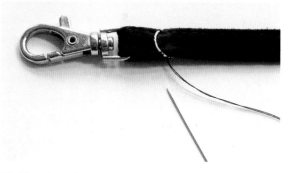

5a. Add swivel clasp and hand-stitch edge.

5b. Thread small ring and sew over seam.

Slide the small ring down over the joint and secure in the same way as in the previous step (5b, 5c). Thread an anchor through a large ring (5d). Insert a small ring into the anchor, stitching it in the same position as you did for the wrist strap. Thread the other strap anchor through the large ring on the wrist strap and add the small ring, stitching it in the same position as the others (5e).

Add the strap

6. Add the strap anchors to the sides of the bag, centering them over the zipper teeth in the valley created by the zipper tape's thinner edges. (Placing the anchors in the valley balances the seam weight along the side edge.) Hand-baste the anchors through the front of the bag only, keeping the back of the bag free (6a). Turn the bag inside out, folding it so the center of the zipper teeth is ¾ inch from the top edge of the bag (the seam allowance will butt up against the fold) and securing with binder clips (6b). Sew the bag side seams using a ¼-inch seam allowance, leaving the zipper open for turning the bag right side out and taking care not to catch the loose strap (6c).

7. Turn the bag right side out and topstitch ⅜ inch from the edge. You are now stitching a French seam in reverse, so the seam ends up on the outside instead of the inside.

> **NOTE** A traditional French seam is one in which the raw edges are enclosed and sewn in two steps. First, sew with the wrong sides together. Trim the seam as needed, then sew with the right sides facing, enclosing the raw edges.

8. For even stitching, use a Hump Jumper in the voids where necessary to balance out the seam height (8a). Tie the threads tails at the beginning and ending of the stitching line. To make a clean finish, thread a needle with the tails and insert in the bag (8b). Decorate the zipper slider with additional rings (8c). The zipper pull needs to be sturdy, so start with a heavy-duty jump ring. Attach it to the slider and insert a large ring before closing. Add a figure-eight connector and crimp. Add the smaller ring, and crimp to finish (8d).

5c. Secure small ring.

5d. Thread anchor through large ring.

5e. Add small ring.

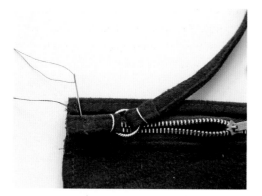

6a. Hand-baste anchors.

6b. Secure seams with binder clips.

6c. Sew seams.

7. Topstitch ⅜ inch from edge.

8a. Use Hump Jumper in voids.

8b. Thread needle with tails.

8c. Decorate zipper slider.

8d. Crimp smaller ring.

Dimensions: 12 inches wide by
7 inches high by 2 inches deep

Seam allowance: ½ inch,
unless otherwise noted

Fibers: Lambskin leather and suede

BEGINNER

Linked-In Handbag

TOOLS AND MATERIALS

Basic Tool Kit (p. 12)

Pattern for link (p. 170)

5 square feet thin leather or
1½ yard non-raveling fabric

¼ yard lining fabric

Size 12 Microtex needle

12-inch invisible zipper
for top edge

Manila file folder

¼-in. hole punch

Fusible interfacing

TEMPLATE

Lining, cut one,
15 inch by 9 inch
(includes ½-inch
seam allowance)

FASHION IS CONSTANTLY recycling ideas into fresh looks. This project revives a cool concept from the 1970s to fold and connect leather or faux leather links to make a handbag. The links join vertically or horizontally, and you can attach more than two and then branch into new directions. This bag is a great way to use up scraps or create something new from old accessories. You can make a bag with solid front and back panels, as shown here, or just from links.

Cut the pieces

1. Determine the link shape (1a). Use the pattern to cut link templates from a manila file folder (you will need about 230 for the bag pictured). Trace the template on the leather's wrong side. Mark the hole location on one link end. After the link is cut, fold it in half across the narrow center, right sides in. Punch ¼-inch holes through both sides at the mark (1b).

2. Cut two 10-inch by 5-inch leather pieces. Apply fusible interfacing to the wrong sides. (The panels pictured shrank to 9¼ inches by 4¼ inches.) To minimize shrinkage, use a press cloth and a dry iron set to medium heat.

3. Punch holes in the panels. You'll connect links to the bag's front and back through 28 holes around each panel's edges. Place the holes ¼ inch from the edges and about ⅞ inch apart.

Make the connections

4. Fold a link in half, wrong sides together. Align the holes (4a). Push a second link through the holes in the first link. Slide it halfway through the holes, then fold it in half, wrong sides together (4b).

5. Repeat to add more links. Keep inserting and folding links to join them together. You can orient the links in the same direction or angle them to make a turn. Add more than one link through a hole to branch off.

Line up the links

6. Put links through all the holes on both panel edges. Start with two links in each corner hole. Add a second row of links around the panels.

7. Join the panels and make a strap. Start at the center sides and join links from the panels with perpendicular links. At a top corner, branch the links over the top edges separately. To make a strap, start a chain at a joined corner of the bag top. When the strap is long enough, join it to the opposite top corner. To reinforce it, weave a leather strip into the strap.

8. Lock the links where the rows converge. At the bag's center bottom, insert an extra link (pictured in red), using it to catch the links' edges in one direction and lock through the links from the other direction. Open the extra link on the bag's wrong side; the opposing pull should hold it tightly, or add a few hand stitches to secure.

9. Add a simple drop-in lining. Cut a 15-inch by 19-inch rectangle with a ½-inch seam allowance. With right sides together, fold the lining rectangle crosswise and press the fold. Using a ½-inch seam allowance, sew the seam across the fold, leaving an 11-inch slot opening for the zipper. Press the seam open and add the zipper behind the opening. Using a ½-inch seam allowance, sew the side seams with right sides together. Fold and align the side seam and bottom fold. Sew 1 inch from the point at a 45-degree angle. Repeat on the other corners. Trim all corners. Turn the boxed lining right side out, and sew to the inner link sides at the bag's top edge. Cover a 2-inch by 2-inch cardboard strip with lining fabric and add to bag to support the bag bottom.

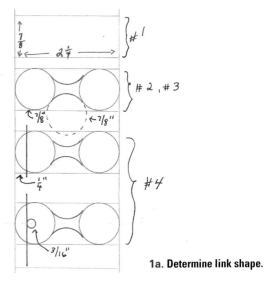

1a. Determine link shape.

1b. Punch holes.

2. Apply fusible interfacing.

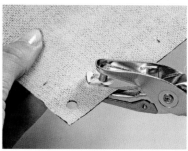
3. Punch holes in panels.

4a. Fold links.

4b. Push through.

5. Add more links.

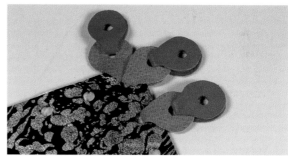
6. Put links through all holes.

7. Join panels.

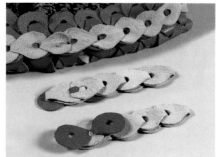
8. Lock links.

9. Sew lining.

Dimensions: 12 inches wide by
9½ inches high by 2½ inches deep

Seam allowance: ⅜ inch,
unless otherwise noted

Fibers: Upholstery fabric with
Mirrabella pearlized lambskin piping

BEGINNER

Sleigh-Bottom Portfolio Clutch

TOOLS AND MATERIALS

Basic Tool Kit (p. 12)
Pattern (p. 170)
⅜ yard upholstery fabric
½ yard lining fabric
1 square foot leather for piping
(to cut 1 inch wide)
Size 12 Microtex needle
12 inches of 1⅜-inch-wide
zipper tape, #10 molded
plastic teeth
#10 zipper slider
Decorative zipper pull
12-inch zipper for inside pocket
50 inches of 8/100-inch-diameter
plastic weed trimmer line
(for piping filler)

THIS PORTFOLIO-SHAPED bag has Old World charm, evoking thoughts of centuries-old weathered boulders and crumbling brick walls. It is trimmed in lambskin leather, and its zipper, which has oversize molded plastic teeth, makes a bold statement. The slider is embellished with a decorative zipper pull that mirrors the design on the fabric, and delicate leather piping provides subtle edging. There are two secrets to getting soft and flexible leather piping that will bend naturally around curves: clipping the seam allowances at very close intervals of ⅛ inch apart and using flexible plastic weed trimmer line, which you can find at your local gardening shop, for the filler.

Cut out the bag

1. To prevent the bag edges from fraying, zigzag stitch or serge all the cut edges. It is important to accurately mark the seamline match points on the sides of the bag where it meets the wedge base as well as the corresponding points on the base. When you assemble the bag you will need them to align the pieces correctly.

Make the leather piping

2. To calculate the amount of piping needed, take one section of the bag and measure the length of the seamline along the sides and bottom edge, starting at the top cut edge, down the side, across the bottom, and up the other side to the top cut edge. On the separate base wedge, measure the seamline on one side only from cut edge to cut edge. Cut the piping 1 inch wide by the length you just measured. Cut the plastic line the same length minus the seam allowances.

3. Before gluing the plastic line to the strips, double-check that they are the correct length. If any plastic line extends beyond the seamlines, trim it off. Use a utility lighter to carefully apply heat to the tips to melt them into a rounded end (3a). Spray temporary adhesive on the back of the leather strips (3b).

4. To create the piping for the bag section, wrap the leather strip around the plastic filler, offsetting the cut edges $\frac{1}{16}$ inch and tucking the ends inside the piping (4a). To make the piping for the base wedge, wrap the strip around the filler, but do not tuck the ends inside, as you did on the bag section. With a sharp pair of scissors, make tiny clips every $\frac{1}{8}$ inch within the seam allowance (4b).

5. Use binder clips to attach the piping to the right side of the bag, placing the piping ends at the seamline on the top edge. Stretch the piping's cut edge around the curves so the corners will cup when the bag is finished (5a). Using a zipper foot, sew the piping to the bag as close to the filler as possible (5b). Attach the piping to the base wedge, extending the piping to the cut ends. Sew in place (5c). With right sides together, attach the base wedge with the piped edge to the side of the bag that has no piping (5d). To further tighten the piping, machine-sew just inside the previous stitching line.

Make the zipper

6. Prepare the zipper for the bag's top edge (the edge across the bag top, including seam allowances, is $12\frac{3}{4}$ inches). Cut the zipper $11\frac{1}{2}$ inches and use chalk to mark the ends with a $\frac{3}{8}$-inch seam allowance. Use side-cutting pliers to remove the plastic molded teeth within the seam allowance. Use a utility lighter to carefully sear the cut edges.

7. Cut four patches $1\frac{3}{4}$ inches square. Sandwich the zipper ends within two squares and sew using a $\frac{3}{8}$-inch seam allowance (7a). Repeat on the other end of the zipper. If your fabric is heavy, use a lighter weight fabric for the square on the back of the zipper (7b).

1. Zigzag stitch all edges.

2. Cut piping and filler.

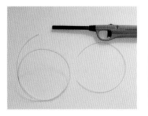
3a. Sear plastic tips.

3b. Use spray adhesive.

4a. Wrap strip around piping.

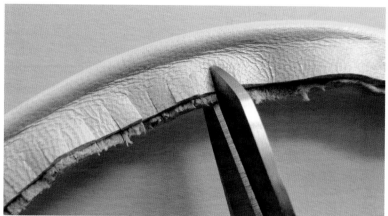

4b. Make tiny clips every ⅛ inch.

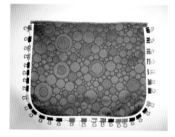

5a. Clip piping to right side of bag.

5b. Sew piping close to filler.

5c. Sew piping to base wedge.

5d. Attach base wedge.

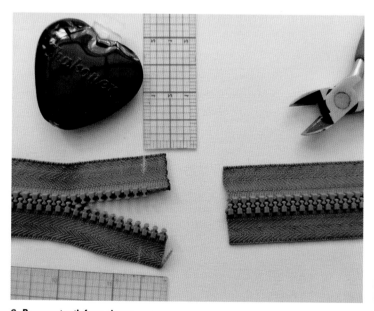

6. Remove teeth from zipper.

7a. Sew zipper ends within two squares.
7b. Back of zipper uses a lightweight fabric.

8. Fold the patches over the zipper ends and trim, cutting the zipper to the same length as the top edge of the bag, then cut the width flush with the zipper side. Zigzag-stitch over edges.

9. With right sides together, place the zipper on the bag and sew with a shy ¼-inch seam (9a). Align the other edge with the zipper tape and sew in the same way (9b).

10. Press the seam allowances away from the zipper and, from the right side, edgestitch close to the fold, catching all the seam allowances. Stitch again ¼ inch away from the first row of stitching (10a). On the side with the piping, end the edgestitching at the piping; do not sew through it (10b).

Sew the bag sides and bottom

11. With right sides together, fold the bag in half so the top edge is at the center of the zipper teeth. Sew the side seams, starting at the top edge and ending at the bottom seamline. Sew the remaining seam on the base wedge to the bottom of the bag, starting and stopping at the seamline.

Make the lining

12. On one side of the lining add a patch pocket with the finished dimensions of 9½ inches wide by 6½ inches high (12a). For the zippered pocket, on the back, mark a window ⁷⁄₁₆ inch high by 9½ inches long. Cut through the center up to ½ inch from the

corners, then cut diagonally into the corners. Press the edges back (you do not have to stabilize fabric that does not fray) (12b). Place the zipper behind the window and sew all around the edge (12c).

13. Before attaching the patch pockets, finish them by lining or turning back the raw edges (13a). Attach the pocket pouch to the zipper (10½-inch by 12-inch rectangle), first sewing one edge of the pouch to the bottom tape, then sewing to the top tape. To complete the pocket, sew the side seams, keeping the bag free. Move the pouch for the zippered pocket out of the way so you don't stitch through it and add the small patch pocket with the finished dimensions of 4¼ inches wide by 4 inches high (13b).

14. Sew the base wedge to one side of the bag, starting and stopping at the seamline match point (14a). Sew the other side of the base to the bag in the same way. Next, sew the side seams, starting at the top edge and stopping at the bottom seamline match point (14b). On the top edge, press down the seam allowance.

Add the lining

15. With the wrong sides facing, secure the bases together, lining up the edges. Stitch within the seam allowances, breaking the stitching at the sides (15a). Turn the bag right side out. Line up the fold on the lining edge with the stitching line on the zipper and hand-stitch (15b). Decorate the zipper pull (15c).

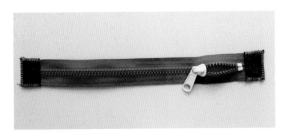

8. Zigzag-stitch over edges.

9a. Align and sew zipper to one edge.

9b. Align other edge and sew zipper.

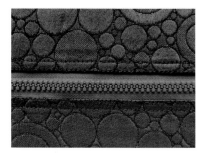

10a. Stitch zipper close to fold and ¼ inch from first row.

10b. End edgestitching at piping.

11. Sew remaining seam on base wedge.

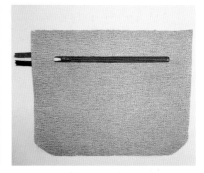

12a. Add patch pocket.

12b. Mark a window for zippered pocket.

12c. Place zipper behind window and sew around.

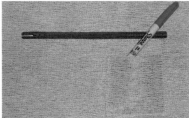

13a. Finish patch pockets before topstitching.

13b. Add small patch pocket.

14a. Sew base wedge to bag.

14b. Sew side seams.

15a. Stitch within seam allowances.

15b. Hand-stitch fold on lining to zipper.

15c. Decorate zipper pull.

Dimensions: 16 inches wide by
12½ inches high by 3 inches deep

Seam allowance: ½ inch,
unless otherwise noted

Fibers: Upholstery fabric trimmed
with pebble-grain garment leather

BEGINNER

Fold-Over Frame Bag

TOOLS AND MATERIALS

Basic Tool Kit (p. 12)
Pattern (p. 171)
½ yard upholstery fabric
3 square feet leather or ¼ yard fabric
½ yard lining for optional overlay
¾ yard fabric for lining and pockets
⅛ yard interfacing
Topstitching thread
Size 16 topstitching needle
Four 9-inch zippers, plastic coil
Decorative clasp
Small piece of bag stiffener
6 inches of 20-gauge wire
11-inch by 4-inch metal purse frame
⅛-inch cotton piping cord
1¼ yards shoelacelike cord
19-inch curved link chain
Two #10-24 by ½ inch ceiling fan
blade screws
Four #10 nylon washers
Two ⁵⁄₃₂-inch by ⅜-inch by
¹⁄₁₆-inch rubber washers
Two #10-24 acorn nuts

TEMPLATES

Leather base, cut one,
3 inch by 36½ inch
Leather center front strip,
cut one, 1⅛ inch by 14½ inch
Tab closure, cut two,
7 inch by 2¼ inch (in leather)

THE SILHOUETTE on this bag is part vintage, part contemporary. When folded over, you can carry it as a clutch or hang it over your arm using the metal chain strap, which is permanently attached to the fold-away hinges. When you are not using the strap, it folds into the bag and is stored in a shallow zippered pocket that prevents it from getting caught within the contents of the bag. In order to stow as much of the strap as possible, you will take apart and alter the zipper so two sliders can zip toward each other, which allows the chain to drop into the middle of the pocket.

Determine the flange length

1. When the metal frame is in the closed position, the gap within the hinge arm will vary depending on frame style. Unless you are using the exact same frame as the one shown, you will need to calculate the length of the extension needed to safely warp around the hinge without preventing the frame from shutting tightly. To determine the flange length, simply measure the distance beyond where the frame needs to sit flush when closed. In the bag pictured, the area between the 1½-inch and 3½-inch marks on the ruler indicates the space into which the flange can be tucked. The maximum flange length on this frame is 4 inches.

Sew the bag

2. Cut the bag without the seam allowances at center front. Clean-finish the cut edges so they won't fray (2a). Cut the bottom band as one long strip (you will cut the corners for the box bottom later). Use scalloping shears to trim one of the long edges, barely shaving off ¹⁄₁₆ inch. Place the band at the base of the bag, aligning the bottom edges. Use topstitching thread to topstitch the band to the bag ¼ inch away from the scalloped edge (2b). With the fabric wrong side up, finish attaching the band to the base, machine-basting the band to the remaining edges ⅛ inch away from the cut edges, and baste around the box corner edges.

3. Finish cutting the box corners on the leather layer (3a). Butt the center front edges together and sew the seam with a zigzag stitch (3b). Cut the cover strip 1⅛ inches wide by 14½ inches long. Use scalloping shears to trim the cover strip on both long edges, cutting off only ¹⁄₁₆ inch on each edge. Place the strip on the bag, centering it over the seam. Use topstitching thread to sew ¼ inch away from the scalloped edge (3c).

4. Make a little paper pattern for each side of the clasp, marking the position for the hook, eye, and prongs. Be sure to trace both sections of the clasp because sometimes the spacing between the prongs can differ between the two segments. On the clasp used here, there was a difference of ⅛ inch.

5. Cut out the patch and transfer the clasp prong position. Use a Crop-A-Dile II to pierce the holes for the prongs. Place the patch on the bag, centering it over the leather strip. Topstitch all around to secure (5a). Use an awl to pierce the fabric to separate the fibers. Add the clasp, pushing the prongs through the holes (5b).

6. Cut a small piece of bag stiffener to reinforce the clasp. Use a Crop-A-Dile II to cut the holes for prongs. Add the stiffener to the wrong side of the bag. To secure, insert a section of wire and twist it together (6a). Cut off the extra wire and make sure the tip ends are flat and tucked away under the twisted wire. Glue a piece of leather over the wire mechanism to ensure it does not tear or wear down the adjacent lining (6b).

7. With right sides together, align the bag's bottom edges and sew the seam. Open the seam, pounding it over a hard surface. Around tight areas that cannot lay flat, place a shaped hard object, like a rock, behind the leather. Small pieces of hardwood are good for straighter edges. From the right side, topstitch on both sides of the seam, sewing ¼ inch from the seam (7a). Fold the bag's corners, aligning the bottom seam with the match point on the side of the bag. Sew the seam, which is 3 inches long (7b).

1. Measure for flange.

2a. Finish cut edges of bag.

2b. Trim with scalloping shears.

3a. Cut box corners.

3b. Zigzag stitch.

3c. Sew seam ¼ inch from scalloped edge.

4. Trace clasp.

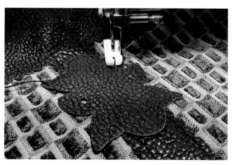

5a. Sew patch.

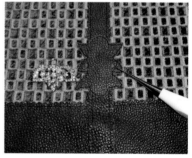

5b. Add clasp.

6a. Secure clasp with wire.

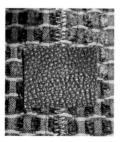

6b. Glue leather over wire.

7a. Topstitch seam.

7b. Sew seam at corners.

Make and add the lining

8. Add the overlay to the right side of the lining, placing the scalloped border 2 inches from the flange top cut edge. Sew the two layers together, following the curve of the small scallops, across their base and adjacent to the large scallops. Secure the overlay to the lining across the body of the bag by sewing vertically at the markings for the center back, sides, and side corners (8a). The underside shows all the stitching that was done to adhere the two layers (8b).

Make the zipper window

9. On the wrong side of the lining, mark a window that is $3/16$ inch high by the length of your zipper teeth ($3/16$ inch does not seem very big, but it is plenty high to accommodate the coil zipper). Staystitch the window using a short stitch length. When you are getting close to the corner, further tighten the stitch length as you make your way around the corner. Add Fray Check at the corner ends, keeping the sealant inside the window. Let it dry.

10. Cut the opening down the middle of the window until you get to the last $3/4$ inch. At that point, cut diagonally into the corners, one thread shy of the staystitching line (you tightened your staystitching to reinforce this point as much as possible) (10a). Press the edges to the wrong side, rolling the staystitching line to the back so it is $1/16$ inch beyond the fold. The width on your window will now be $5/16$ inch, which is wide enough to accommodate the coil zipper (10b, 10c).

Modify the zipper

11. Remove the two top stoppers from the first zipper. Insert a brass stiletto under the stopper to loosen it a bit until there is enough room to insert the needle-nose pliers. Use pliers to remove the stoppers (11a). From the second zipper, remove the bottom stopper by inserting the stiletto under the staplelike points on the zipper stopper and loosening until you can get a hold of it with needle-nose pliers. Use the pliers to straighten out the prongs until they are vertical. Carefully remove the stopper; try not to bend or break the prongs. Set the stopper aside. Remove the slider and insert it into the first zipper (11b).

12. Insert the stopper you just removed from the second zipper at the base of the coil teeth. Use the pliers to bend the prongs. Treat the zipper as if it had just one slider (12a). (This zipper will be used for the second pocket and will not be shown in subsequent steps.) Place the zipper behind the window and pin to secure (12b, 12c).

13. From the right side, sew the zipper to the window, stitching close to the folded edge. For the pocket pouch cut a rectangle as wide as the zipper length and twice as long as the pocket depth needed (13a on p. 48). Pin the rectangle to the zipper tape's lower edge, keeping the bag layer free. You first pin it to the lower tape instead of the top tape so you can understitch the lower part of the pocket before attaching the other end of the rectangle. The understitching keeps all the seam allowances from popping out of the pocket. Be sure to pin the pocket to the zipper tape only and leave the lining free (13b, 13c on p. 48).

8a. Sew overlay to lining.

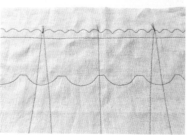
8b. Underside of two layers.

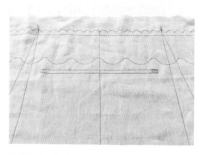
9. Mark window on wrong side of lining.

10a. Cut diagonally into window corners.

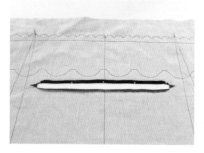
10b. Width of window (wrong side).

10c. Width of window (right side).

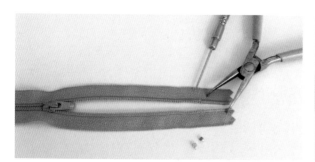
11a. Remove stoppers with needle-nose pliers.

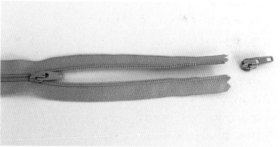
11b. Insert slider into first zipper.

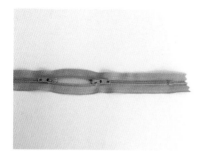
12a. Insert stopper.

12b. Pinned zipper behind window (right side).

12c. Pinned zipper behind window (wrong side).

14. With the pocket facing down toward the feed dogs and using a zipper foot, sew the seam, stitching as close as possible to the visible line of stitching (14a). Although the zipper is securely attached behind the window with two rows of stitching, the tiny seam allowance can still fray with wear, so encase the cut edges using a zigzag stitch (14b). Press all the seam allowances away from the zipper teeth, and stitch the pocket close to the fold though all layers, keeping the bag layer free (14c). Bring the other edge of the rectangle up to meet the zipper tape's upper edge (14d). Pin the rectangle to the zipper tape's upper edge, keeping the bag layer free (14e). Sew the pocket to the zipper in the same manner as you did for the lower edge (14f). Align the pocket's side edges and pin together (14g). To stitch the pocket sides, begin sewing at the zipper corners (14h).

15. Stitch as close as possible to the visible line of stitching at the window corners, then stitch back and forth a few times to secure the triangle at the pocket corners. Continue stitching down the side of the pocket using a ⅜-inch seam allowance. Repeat on the other side of the pocket, except you will need to start stitching the pocket at the bottom folded edge and work your way up to the window. With right sides together, sew the lining's center front seam. Press the seam open. Centering over the seam, make the shallow zipper pocket for the metal chain strap in the same way you made the other pocket.

16. Use interfacing at all the inside corners along the upper edge on both the bag and the lining. Staystitch the corners, reducing the stitch length quite a bit in the immediate vicinity of the corner. Clip into the corner to within a couple of threads of the stitching line. Add Fray Check to the cut. With right sides together, sew the lining to the bag all around the upper edge. Trim the outside corners diagonally. Turn right side out, press, and edgestitch the top edge.

17. Make the tab for the hook section of the clasp as pictured. The tab and facing are cut 2¼ inches by 7 inches, and the bag stiffener to reinforce the clasp is cut 1¾ inches by 1 inch. Transfer the prong placement to the back of the tab and to the bag stiffener. Cut the holes in both (17a on p. 50). Before proceeding, you will need to allow enough clearance between the hook and the tab layers to be able to comfortably insert the clasp into the eye. To reduce the bulk in the area under the hook, remove part of the stiffener, cutting away as much as possible without weakening it. Insert the clasp prongs through the holes in the tab. Add a dab of leathercraft cement to the tab and stiffener, wait a few minutes until it becomes cloudy and tacky, and glue in place (17b on p. 50). Insert a small piece of wire through

13a. Cut pocket pouch.

13b. Pin pocket pouch.

13c. Do not pin lining.

14a. Sew seam.

14b. Encase with zigzag stitch.

14c. Stitch pocket close to fold.

14d. Bring up rectangle edge.

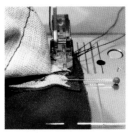

14e. Pin rectangle to zipper tape's upper edge.

14f. Sew pocket to zipper.

14g. Sew pocket side edges.

14h. Sew pocket sides from zipper corners.

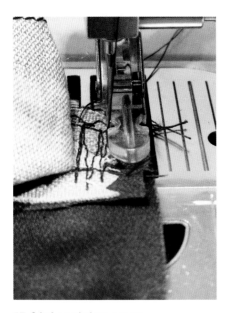

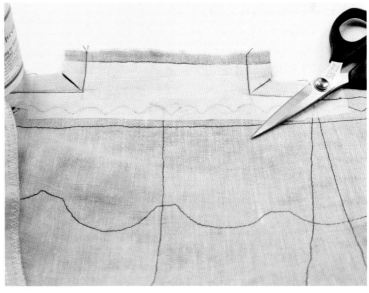

15. Stitch at window corners.

16. Clip into corners.

both prongs. Use pliers to twist the wire and cut off any excess. Tuck the cut ends toward the stiffener (17c).

18. Cut a small piece of leather barely large enough to cover the wires. To keep the bulk to a minimum, cut away the area under the hook and the prong holes so that the patch can sit as flat as possible on the back of the clasp (18a). Glue the patch over the wire housing (18b). Use the foam brush to spread leathercraft cement on both the tab and the facing (18c). Let it sit for a few minutes, until the cement becomes cloudy and tacky (18d).

19. Aligning all edges, glue the two sections together. Before the glue dries, push the facing away from the hook as much as possible so there is enough clearance for the hook to function properly (19a). Let the glue dry. Use scalloping shears to trim the tab on all sides (19b). Place the tab at the center back and sew the last 2 inches, forming a box pattern and taking care not to catch the lining (19c).

20. With right sides together, sew the bottom edge on the lining, leaving an opening for turning right side out (20a). With right sides together, align the bottom seam with the match point on the side, and pin (20b). Draw a 3-inch seamline across the box. Sew over the drawn line (20c).

Add the metal frame

21. The bag top edge is finished and ready to be glued to the frame. Only a portion of the top edge will be inserted into the channel in the frame. The remainder of the length goes around the hinge arm, but only a small section can actually attach to it. That section has been extended with a flange that will wrap around the hinge arm (21a). When the frame shown is fully opened, the span on the hinge arm is 7 inches (21b).

22. Center the frame on the bag and use thread marks to transfer the frame edges to the bag. Working on one side of the frame at a time, add small dots of glue to the channel. Go easy on the glue so it does not ooze when you push the fabric into it. Starting at one end of the frame, align the thread mark with the edge of the frame and push the fabric into the channel. Stuff the fabric for a couple of inches, then move to the other edge of the frame, align the thread mark with the frame edge, and stuff the fabric. Keep stuffing the fabric, alternating a little bit on each side and working your way toward the middle of the frame. Keep a damp cloth nearby and frequently check for any seepage. Insert the other side into the frame in the same way.

17a. Cut holes on one tab and the stiffener.

17b. Push clasp prongs through holes.

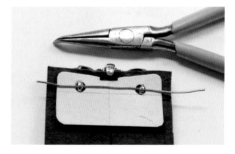

17c. Secure clasp with wire.

18a. Cut leather patch to cover wires.

18b. Glue patch over wires.

18c. Brush cement on tab and facing.

18d. Cloudy and tacky cement.

19a. Push facing away from hook.

19b. Trim tab with scalloping shears.

19c. Sew tab, forming box pattern.

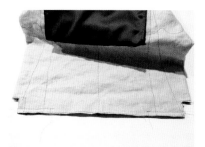

20a. Sew bottom edge on lining.

20b. Align bottom seam, and pin.

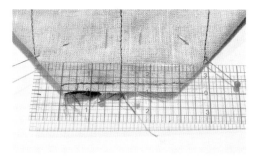

20c. Draw seamline and sew over it.

21a. Frame and channel.

21b. Fully open frame.

22. Add dots of glue to channel.

23. The frame has been glued to the bag's top edge (23a). The fabric alone is not thick enough to totally fill the space within the channel in the frame, but stuffing a cotton cord between the bag and lining makes it nice and snug. It is best to begin with a narrow cord, such as ⅛-inch piping cord, because there are sections of the frame where the channel is narrower, such as at the clasp point, which cannot accommodate the same thickness as other parts of the channel. A dental pick is ideal for tightly packing the cord into the channel (23b).

24. Go through the opening in the lining, pull out and align the corresponding corners, and tie them together using the thread tails (24a). Turn the bag with the lining side out and hand-stitch the opening at the bottom edge of the lining (24b). Wrap the sides of the bag around the hinge and hand-sew the edge to the bag, going only through the lining (24c, 24d, 24e).

Make the chain strap

25. Use a utility lighter to sear the cut end on the shoelacelike cord (25a). Insert the cord in and out of the chain, traveling with it in the hollow of the link curve (25b). To prevent the chain from snaking all over the table, anchor it with a cloth weight. When you get to the end of the chain, turn around and weave back to where you began (25c).

26. Once you finish the weaving, go back and check that there is enough ease in the cord and it is not woven too tight, otherwise the chain will kink. Cut the cord and seal the end with the lighter. Butt the cut ends and hand-sew together. Cover the joint with a scrap of the lining (26a). Work the seam up the chain a couple of inches so it is not right at the end. Maneuver the cord until the weaving is uniform (26b).

Attach the chain strap

27. Connect the chain to the metal loops on the hinged frame using screws, washers, and acorn nuts. The plastic washers buffer the metal loops of the foldaway hinge, and the rubber washer cushions the curvature on the chain link (27a). In the bag shown here, a charm mirroring the bag's silhouette hangs from the chain to disguise the seam (27b).

23a. Frame glued to top edge.

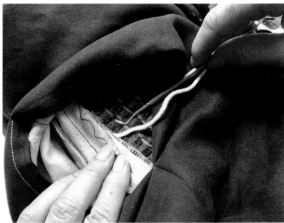

23b. Go through opening in lining and pack cord into channel.

24a. Tie corners together with thread tails.

24b. Hand-stitch opening at bottom of lining.

24c. Wrap sides of bag around hinge.

24d. Hand-sew edge to bag.

24e. Sew only through lining.

25a. Sear cut end of cord.

25b. Insert cord in and out of chain.

25c. Weave back to beginning.

26a. Cover joint with lining scrap.

26b. Maneuver cord.

27a. Connect chain to metal loops.

27b. Use charm to disguise seam.

Dimensions: 12 inches wide
by 19 inches high

Seam allowance: ⅜ inch,
unless otherwise noted

Fiber: Croc-embossed patent leather

BEGINNER

Trendsetter

TOOLS AND MATERIALS

Basic Tool Kit (p. 12)

Pattern (p. 172)

6 square feet leather or
⅝ yard fabric

¾ yard lining fabric

Fusible interfacing

Size 14 Microtex needle

Two 1-inch D-rings

Two 3-inch swivel snap hooks

Adjustable buckle slider (optional)

One ½-inch swivel snap hook

2 split rings

10-inch chain

1 closed ring

TEMPLATE

Loop for D-ring, cut one,
2½ inch by 1 inch (in leather)

FOR THIS SOFT leather sack with a cutout handle, you can use any type of leather or suede, or even try a sturdy fabric such as brocade, denim, or melton. (The version pictured is made from reptile-textured patent leather.) The bag sews up in about two hours, and crafting a custom leather-strip tassel takes another hour or so. The final result is a showstopper: The bag can be tucked over the shoulder through the cutout armhole, or you can use the long strap to sling it across your body messenger-style.

55

Cut and sew the bag

1. Cut the bag and lining, but don't cut the armhole in the lining yet. Cut the flange leather loop, and slip it through a D-ring (1a). Cut a 1-inch slit in the bag where indicated. Slip the flange loop into the slit, open the flange, then topstitch around the slit through both layers (1b).

2. While the bag is still flat, stabilize the seamlines of the bag with ½-inch bias fusible interfacing strips. With wrong sides together, machine-baste the leather to the lining at ¼ inch from the edge along the unfinished upper and sides edges, and down to the midway opening. Machine-baste around the armholes. Cut out the armholes in the lining (the photo shows the lining pulled out).

3. To bind the edges, cut a 1-inch by 42-inch strip for the upper edge, and a 1-inch by 48-inch strip for both armholes. Use binder clips to hold the binding strips in place as you sew them. To attach the other D-ring, use a 1-inch by 2½-inch strip for the loop. Sew the loop with the D-ring to the seamline where indicated. With wrong sides together, sew the leather at the bottom and side seam up to the midway opening, using a ⅜-inch seam allowance. With wrong sides together, sew the lining at the bottom; leave the side seam open for turning. Turn the bag right side out and slipstitch the lining closed.

Add the details

4. Cut a 2-inch strip of leather to your desired strap length, plus 2 inches for attaching to the snap hooks. Lightly brush rubber cement on the wrong side. Fold both long ends until they meet in the center. Let dry.

5. Attach the snap hooks. Fold each short end over a 3-inch snap hook and sew in place. Cut two 2-inch strips, glue and fold as in step 4, then use them to cover the strap's cut ends; sew in place.

   NOTE To make the strap adjustable, add a buckle slider before you attach the snap hooks.

6. Cut fringe to build a tassel. Use the rotary cutter to cut a 10½-inch by 8-inch rectangle. At ¼-inch intervals, cut along the height, stopping each cut 1 inch from the top edge.

7. Assemble the hardware (½-inch snap hook, split ring, chain, split ring, closed ring). Cut a ½-inch by 2½-inch strip for the attaching loop. Slip the leather loop through the closed ring and sew to secure. Add rubber cement to the top edge of the fringe, then tightly roll it around the leather loop; slipstitch around the top edge to secure. Wrap a piece of chain around the top. Clip the tassel to one of the bag's D-rings.

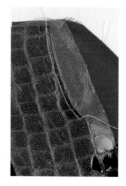

1a. Cut loop and slip through D-ring.

1b. Slip loop inside slit.

2. Machine-baste leather to lining.

3. Use binder clips to hold the layers.

4. Fold long ends until they meet in the center.

5. Attach snap hooks.

6. Cut fringe.

7. Roll fringe.

Dimensions: 13 inches wide by
8½ inches high by 2½ inches deep

Seam allowance: ⅜ inch,
unless otherwise noted

Fiber: Pearlized upholstery leather

BEGINNER

Trapezoid Netbook Case

TOOLS AND MATERIALS

Basic Tool Kit (p. 12)

Pattern (p. 173)

3 square feet leather or
⅝ yard fabric

⅝ yard lining

Size 14 leather needle

Size 18 leather needle

At least 14 inches of zipper tape,
#5 metal teeth

#5 zipper slider

9-inch invisible zipper

Gum tragacanth

Kitchen cabinet handle
with holes 5 inches apart

Two ⅜-inch screws

2 washers

TEMPLATES

Lining, cut one,
16½ inch by 23 inch

Patch pocket, cut one,
16¼ inch by 6 inch

THIS BAG IS SIZED to fit a standard netbook computer, but you can easily scale it up or down to custom fit a larger laptop or a tablet device. The lining walls can be interfaced with a layer of foam padding to provide a safe cushion for your gadget. The top and bottom edges are reinforced with facings that are backed with a stiffener. Topping the bag is an easy-to-grip kitchen cabinet handle. Inside you will add one patch pocket and one with an invisible zipper; together they provide ample space to store all your extras securely.

Prepare and add the zipper

1. Use pinking or scalloping shears to trim off the ³⁄₈-inch seam allowance, if one was added. Use a small paintbrush to apply the gum tragacanth along the decorative edges. Let dry about an hour, then apply a second coat. On the back of the leather transfer the match points (green and red dots on pattern), using a dot to indicate the center and the corners of each box.

2. Start with a longer zipper length than needed. Remove the stopper and slider and save them for later. Cut the zipper into a 14-inch length and pull it apart. Use side-cutting pliers to snip off the teeth within the seam allowance. Be sure to cut the same number of teeth at each edge. Sear the cut edges with a utility lighter so they don't ravel.

3. Place one edge of the bag on the zipper tape, aligning the decorative edge ⅛ inch away from the teeth. Using a zipper foot, size 14 leather needle, and two threads through the needle, sew ⅛ inch away from the top edge of the decorative edge. Add the second section of the zipper to the other edge of the bag in the same way, paying attention to the orientation of the teeth (see "Security Pouch," p. 28)

Prepare the facings

4. Cut the bag stiffener without seam allowances, a 2½-inch by 13-inch strip for the bottom and a 1½-inch by 11-inch strip for the top. Add a few strips of double-face tape to the stiffener. Peel back the paper and attach it to the facing's wrong side. Add double-face tape to the seam allowances on the long edges just shy of the short ends. Peel back the tape and fold the seam allowances over the stiffener edge. Try to keep the tape out of the stitching line as much as possible because it will gum up the needle. If you must sew through it, wipe the needle every few inches so you won't have to remove it for cleaning.

5. On the back of the top facing, mark the placement for the handle screws, and use a Crop-A-Dile II to cut the holes (5a). (Cabinet handles are normally 5 inches apart, but double-check yours.) For bulk-free and smoothly finished corners, trim the seam allowance on the facings' short T ends and partially fold the corners before sewing the facings to the bag. Don't be tempted to trim the corner, as seen on the left side of photo 5b, because what seems obvious is not always the best solution. Instead, cut off a wedge in the shape of a slanted L, cutting the bottom of the L parallel to the short end on the stiffener, as seen on the right side of the photo 5b. Add a small piece of double-face tape. This is the angle at which the corners will eventually fold. The seam allowances will be pushed away from the seamline so there will be absolutely no bulk at the corners (5c).

Add the facings and sew seams

6. Add a few strips of double-face tape to the bottom facing's wrong side. Peel back the paper and place the facing over the bottom of the right side of the bag. Use the size 18 leather needle and two threads through the needle to sew the long edges, topstitching close to the fold through all layers, starting and stopping at the seamline (6a). Pull all the threads to the back, and tie (6b).

7. Add the top facing to the bag and stitch in the same way you did for the bottom. Finish cutting the holes for the handle screws, going through the existing holes on the facing. The screws used for attaching the handle are longer than the layers, so you will need to build up the layers with a piece of bag stiffener to secure the handle nice and tight. For each screw, cut a scrap of stiffener, pierce the hole, and glue to the bag on the wrong side, matching the holes. Insert the zipper slider. Close up the ends of the zipper tape, butting the edges, and hand-stitch together. Attach the zipper stopper.

1. Trim edges.

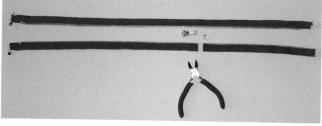

2. Snip teeth.

3. Sew ⅛ inch from top edge of decorative edge.

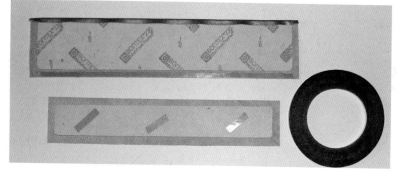

4. Add double-face tape.

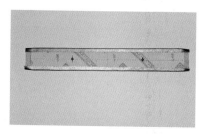

5a. Cut holes for handle screws.

5b. Do not trim corner.

5c. Fold corners.

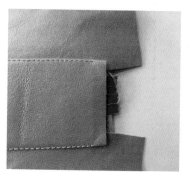

6a. Topstitch long edges.

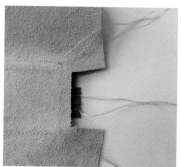

6b. Pull threads to back and tie.

7. Add top facing and sew.

8. With right sides together, sew the side seams, taking care not to catch any of the facing edges (8a). Turn the bag right side out. Add a small piece of double-face tape at the corner edge of the bottom facing seam allowance (8b). The dot is the center of the box and thus the center bottom of the bag. When you turn the bag wrong side out to sew the corner, the dot will be aligned with the side seam.

9. Peel the paper and fold the corners at a 45-degree angle, tucking the tip ends down between the stiffener and the bag (9a). Turn the bag wrong side out. Match the side seam with the dot at center bottom and stitch the seam, sewing across the corner from fold to fold, leaving long thread tails. Stitch parallel to the stiffener edge, but not through it. Repeat with the other corner. Fold the top facing ends and sew the top box corners in the same way as you did on the bottom box corners. The photo shows the top box corner ready to be sewn (9b). Then turn the bag right side out and inspect your perfect corner (9c).

Make and add the lining

10. The bag lining fits within a 16½-inch-wide by 21½-inch-long rectangle, but to insert the invisible zipper you will need to start with a longer piece to allow for the seam allowances, so cut it 16½ inches wide and 23 inches long. Cut this rectangle into two pieces of 6 inches and 17 inches. Insert the invisible zipper between the two sections. On the bag pictured, I used a 9-inch invisible zipper and installed it off to one side. The finished opening is 8 inches and the pocket was cut to 9 inches wide by 13 inches long. Lay the pattern on the lining, placing the invisible zipper seam 5¼ inches from the edge of the pattern. Cut the lining.

11. On the lining wrong side, mark the handle position and the placement of the patch pocket center point. (The patch pocket is placed on the wall opposite the invisible zipper pocket.) Mark the box corners, using a dot to indicate the center and the corners of

each box. (See the white dots in photo 12a, which mark the corners of each box.) On the lining wrong side, use interfacing at the point where the center of the pocket will be sewn and the area where the holes will be pierced for the handle screws. Cut a rectangle 6 inches high by the width of the bag, using the widest part (16¼ inches). Hem one long edge using a ⅜-inch double hem (press back ⅜ inch, then press back another ⅜ inch) and press back the seam allowance on the other long edge. Add the rectangle, aligning the short sides with the bag sides. The extra fullness at the top edge will create depth. Sew the pocket on the three sides. Sew down the center of the pocket, splitting it into two equal compartments. Zigzag stitch all around the edges to clean finish.

12. Press back the seam on the zipper edges and, with right sides together, sew the side seams (12a). Box the corners. Bring the cut edges together, aligning the side seam with the mark at the center of the box. Sew the seam from the dot at the fold to the dot at the other fold, leaving long thread tails (12b).

13. With wrong sides together and fronts facing each other, place the bag on top of the lining. Matching the box corners, align the box's cut edges, and tie the threads together. Trim the tied tails. Turn the bag right side out and baste the lining to the zipper.

Add the handle

14. Smooth out the lining to get it ready for cutting the holes. Finish cutting the holes by going through the existing holes on the facing (14a). Screw the handle to the top, using a washer and screw (14b, 14c). Turn the bag with the lining side out and hand-sew the lining to the zipper tape, then turn the bag right side out (14d).

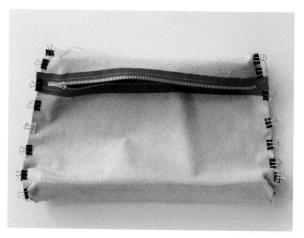

8a. Sew side seams.

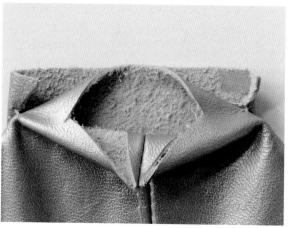

8b. Add double-face tape to corner edge.

9a. Fold corners.

9b. Top box corner ready to be sewn.

9c. Perfect corner.

11. Sew pocket.

12a. Sew side seams.

12b. Sew from dot to dot.

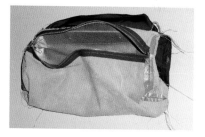

13. Align box cut edges and tie threads together.

14a. Finish cutting holes for handle.

14b. Screw handle to top.

14c. Washers and screws.

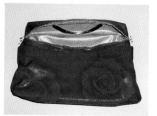

14d. Hand-sew lining to zipper tape.

Dimensions: 10 inches square

Seam allowance: ½ inch,
unless otherwise noted

Fibers: Heavy silk satin and
Mirrabella metallic lambskin

BEGINNER

1940s Hobo Wristlet

TOOLS AND MATERIALS

Basic Tool Kit (p. 12)

Pattern (p. 175)

½ yard lightweight cotton batting

½ yard muslin

2 square feet leather or ½ yard fabric

½ yard lining

Size 12 Microtex needle

Topstitching-weight silk thread for
the quilting

14 inches of zipper tape,
#5 metal teeth

#5 zipper slider

7-inch zipper, plastic coil

½-inch wide plastic headband

Rhinestone setter tool

Swarovski rhinestones

TEMPLATES

Lining, cut one, 15¼-inch square
(includes ½-inch seam allowance)

Handle cover, cut one,
1⅞ inch by 16 inch
(in leather; includes two
⅝-inch seam allowance)

THIS BAG IS MADE from buttery soft Mirrabella lambskin, heavy silk satin, and a leather-covered handle. The body is quilted in a simple crosshatch grid, and the intersections are accented with twinkling Swarovski® rhinestones. The starry theme carries through to the lining, which is cut from a silver-frosted illusion. The quilting, which adds stability, also beefs up an otherwise drapey fabric into an appropriate weight. The high contrast between the leather and silk accentuates the scalloped edging on the bands, and tiny box corners define the points. The bag folds flat, and when propped up turns into a four-pointed star.

65

Make the quilting

1. The fabric square will shrink from all the cross-hatch stitching, so for a 12-inch finished quilted square with a ½-inch seam allowance, begin with a piece of fabric that is at least 13¼ inches. On a large piece of tissue paper, draw a 13-inch square. Use a different color ink to draw lines through the center vertically and horizontally. From the center points draw parallel lines 1 inch apart in both directions. Cut around the paper, leaving a ½-inch border. Stack the muslin, cotton batting, bag fabric, and tissue paper template. Make sure the layers are smooth. If they are not, iron them.

2. Hand-baste the layers together with silk thread, which is much easier to remove, even when the needle sews through the core. Baste around the perimeter, across the centers, and diagonally corner to corner (2a). Sew the layers together, starting with the center row. To prevent the layers from shifting, sew the center row and the perpendicular one, then continue sewing from the center out, alternating sides. For pronounced stitching lines, use a longer stitch length (8 stitches/inch), topstitching thread, or two threads through the needle (2b).

3. If you quilted the rows evenly at 1 inch apart, the last row of stitching around the perimeter will be at 12 inches. This 12-inch measurement is important because it is your seamline and also the matching points for the bands. Be aware of the finished measurements because the size of your square is related to the dimensions of the bands.

4. Remove the basting lines and carefully tear the tissue paper (4a). It is tempting to cut all those thread tails, but leave them. Unless you secured the stitching at the beginning and end of each row, you run the risk of the stitches coming undone at the edges (4b).

Make the side bands

5. Use scalloping shears to trim the long edges on the side bands, shaving off a mere ¹⁄₁₆ inch at each edge. Do the same on the top band's long edges (5a). With right sides together, fold the bottom corner and sew using a ¼-inch seam allowance, which is the width of one scallop. Repeat with the other band (5b). Tie all loose threads, thread them on a needle, and bury the tails within the skin.

6. Fold the bag square in half to locate the center point, which will become the bottom of your bag. Match the seam on the side band with the center point on the bag, placing the scallop tip ¼ inch beyond the bag seamline. Use a small piece of ³⁄₈-inch double-face tape to hold the match points. This line of stitching is being sewn directly on top of the seamline on the bag.

7. Begin sewing at the bottom of the bag, stitching ¼ inch away from the tip of the scallop. Sew to the top edge of the bag (7a). Return back to the bottom and finish sewing the side band (7b). On the other side of the bag, sew the side band the same way.

1. Make quilting.

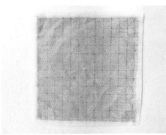

2a. Hand-baste layers.

2b. Sew from center out.

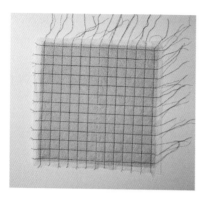

3. Checked finished measurements.

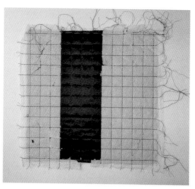

4a. Tear tissue paper.

4b. Leave thread tails.

5a. Trim long edges on side bands.

5b. Fold and sew bottom corner on side bands.

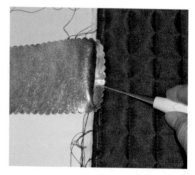

6. Match side band seam with center point on bag.

7a. Stitch ¼ inch from tip of scallop.

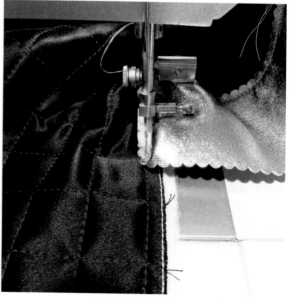

7b. Finish sewing side band.

Make the top band

8. The side bands extend beyond the top edge of the bag. This reinforces the handle ends at a secondary point along the side bands because the extension allows the band to reach up to the handle ends (8a). On the back of the top band, draw a rectangle, ⅝ inch wide by 12 inches long, centered on the band. Cut the window (8b). Cut the zipper 14 inches long (8c). On the side that you just cut, use side-cutting pliers to snip off a few teeth so they do not interfere with the stitching line (8d). Use a utility lighter to carefully sear the cut edges to prevent the zipper tape from fraying (8e).

Make the handle

9. Cut the leather strip to cover the headband handle. This should measure three times the width plus ¹⁄₁₆ inch to allow for trimming the edge with scalloping shears, and 1¼ inches more for seam allowances. The ½-inch-wide headband has some depth, so the leather is cut 1⅞ inches wide by 16 inches long, and after scalloping one edge it becomes 1¾ inches wide. Apply ⅜-inch double-face tape all around the outer curve.

10. Align the leather's straight border with one edge on the headband, peel back the tape's paper a small section at a time, and run your fingers over the top curve to smooth out the leather. Add another strip

of ⅜-inch double-face tape all around the inside curve. Peel back the paper and fold the leather over the inside curve. Finger press.

11. Add more ⅜-inch double-face tape all around the outer curve. Peel back the paper and begin folding the leather over the top, aligning the tips on the scallops with the edge on the headband. The leather is pliable, so tug on it until the tip of the scallops meet the edge. When taping on a surface that is not flat, you will need to manipulate the leather a small section at a time, so add the double-face tape in small increments. You can then peel the sections one by one. Do not tape areas prematurely.

12. Insert the zipper slider and mark the center point on the zipper. Center the handle, placing the plastic tip ends ¼ inch away from where you will be stitching. Don't sew too close to the plastic tips; you want the handle to remain flexible. Sew the handle to the zipper tape (12a). Apply ⅛-inch double-face tape to the zipper edges, making sure it is far enough away that you don't stitch through it in the next step. Peel back the paper and insert the top band, making sure the zipper is centered within the window (12b). Using a zipper foot, stitch the band to the zipper tape (12c, 12d). With right sides together, fold the ends and sew using a ¼-inch seam allowance, which is the width of one scallop. Tie all loose threads, thread them on a needle, and bury the tails within the skin (12e).

8a. Side bands extend beyond top edge of bag.

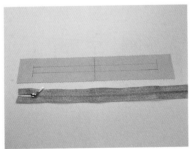

8b. Draw rectangle.

8c. Cut zipper.

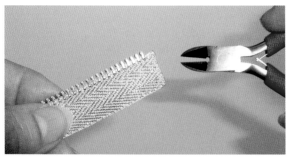

8d. Snip teeth.

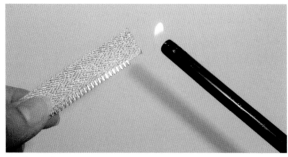

8e. Sear edges.

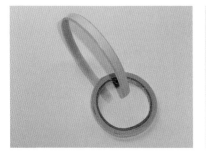

9. Add double-face tape to headband outer curve.

10. Fold leather over inside curve.

11. Fold leather over outer curve.

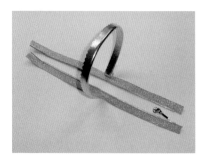

12a. Sew handle to zipper tape.

12b. Insert band into zipper tape.

12c. Use a zipper foot to sew band to zipper tape.

12d. Top band stitched to zipper tape.

12e. Tie threads and bury tails.

ORIENTING THE ZIPPER

You can fold the square in either direction. For the bag pictured, I placed the zipper pocket opening parallel to the fold. Using the folding orientation in step 15, the zippered pocket ends up in the bag on the side perpendicular to the bag opening edge. If you want to place the zippered pocket so it ends up parallel to the bag opening, simply fold the lining square in the other direction, so the side seams become parallel to the zippered pocket opening. If you fold it in this manner, be sure the pocket opening is as close as possible to the upper edge, so you have room to unzip it easily.

Add the top band

13. Locate the center points on the bag and match them to the seams on the top band, placing the scallop tip ¼ inch beyond the seamline. This line of stitching will be sewn directly on top of the seamline on the bag. Use a small piece of ⅜-inch double-face tape to hold the match points (13a). Stitch the band to the bag ¼ inch away from the tip of the scallop. Start sewing at the seam junction on the band (13b), making sure the handle is centered on the side band. Sew to the other seam junction, then stop—you will need to align the other side of the handle, and this is easier if you remove the bag from the sewing machine bed. If you opened the zipper in the previous step, close it up so you can accurately center the handle on the side band and ensure the side bands will end up directly across from each. On the inside of the bag, secure the handle ends to the extension on the side band, butting the edges (trim if necessary) and hand-stitching together. Be careful not to catch the bag.

Make the corners and embellish

14. To form the box corners, fold the bag flat to form natural triangles at the corners (14a). The box is 1 inch. Center the seam on the triangle and from the tip point on the triangle, measure up ½ inch, and draw a 1-inch line across. Sew the seam following the drawn line and leave long thread tails. To secure the stitching, tie each end. Repeat with the other three corners (14b). Use a setting tool to add a rhinestone at every other quilted corner or as desired (14c).

Make the lining

15. Add a zippered pocket, following step 16 in "North–South Convertible Tote" on p. 112. Fold the lining square in half and sew the seam at each end; see "Orienting the Zipper" at left for options. Two of the box corners are made at the bottom corners and two are made at the top opening edge, at the center. To make the corners on the top edge, you will need to sew a short seam before making the box. To find the center, fold the edge, matching the side seams. From the fold, sew a 1⅛-inch seam. Repeat on the other edge. Mark and sew the four boxes in the same way you did on the bag corners (15a, 15b).

16. With wrong sides together, place the lining on top of the bag (16a). Make sure the zipper is parallel to the opening on the lining. Remember that this is a square, so you don't want to tie the corners just to find out the openings do not align. Tie the corresponding box corners together (16b).

17. Turn the bag so the lining is facing out and pin the lining to the zipper edge. Hand-stitch the two layers together. Turn the bag right side out.

13a. Match center points on bag to seams on band.

13b. Sew one side of the band to the bag.

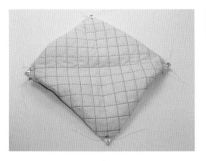

14a. Fold to form triangles at corners.

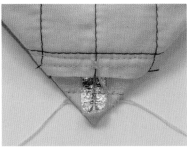

14b. Sew seams, leaving long tails.

14c. Add rhinestones at corners.

15a. Sew 1⅛ inches from fold.

15b. Mark and sew four boxes.

16a. Place lining on top of bag.

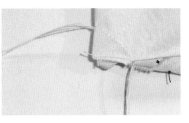

16b. Tie corners together.

17. Hand-stitch layers together.

Dimensions: 13 inches wide by
5½ inches high by 2¼ inches deep

Seam allowance: ½ inch,
unless otherwise noted

Fiber: Plastic-laminated nylon

BEGINNER

Clutch with Padded Bar Handle

TOOLS AND MATERIALS

Basic Tool Kit (p. 12)

Pattern (p. 176)

¾ yard fabric

½ yard lining

¼ yard cotton batting

¼ yard muslin

16 inches of zipper tape,
#3 metal teeth

#3 zipper slider

9-inch zipper, plastic coil
(for inside pocket)

2 yards of ⅛-inch ribbon

Two ¾-inch by 12-inch pieces
bag stiffener

Two ¾-inch by 12-inch pieces
high-density foam

Bodkin

THIS SWEET LITTLE bag features an ergonomic built-in bar handle, which offers a natural grip that feels comfortable in the palm of your hand. High-density foam, beveled and backed with bag stiffener, gives the bar handle body, depth, and dimension. The bag is made from rubber-coated nylon fabric, which repels water and wards off stains. One side is green and the other is gray; the lining uses the gray side. The soft structure is achieved with underlining. The ruffle and top zipper closure are backed with muslin and the main bag is backed with cotton batting. You can make this simple yet versatile shape out of a variety of textiles and supple leathers. For a hands-free bag, simply add a strap.

Prepare the underlining

1. Add the batting to the bag front, back, and gusset, staystitching the two layers together within the seam allowance. Add the muslin to the top band/ruffle and zipper lips in the same way.

Sew the bag

2. With right sides together, sew the bag from front to back along the bottom edge. On a piece of ribbon mark the finished bottom width at 13 inches. Place the first mark at ½ inch and the second mark 13 inches away (2a). Place the ribbon over the seam allowance and zigzag stitch over it, keeping the ribbon free of stitching (2b). Draw up the ribbon until the marks line up with the seam allowance (2c). Secure the ribbon ends within the seam allowance. Trim away the excess ribbon (2d).

Pleat and tuck the top edge

3. Form a 1-inch box pleat at the center front. On each side of the center front make five ½-inch tucks, spaced 1 inch apart, and pin. Machine-sew to secure.

Prepare the padded bar

4. From the bag stiffener cut two strips, each 12 inches long by ¾ inch wide. Use a serrated knife to cut two strips from the high-density foam, each 12 inches long by ¾ inch wide by ⅝ inch high. Bevel two of the long edges on the ⅝-inch side (4a). Glue the foam to the stiffener and wrap it with a 1-inch-wide strip of cotton batting (4b).

Prepare the top band ruffle

5. With wrong sides together, fold the ruffle along the foldline (the foldline is not at the halfway point). Sew part of the short seam, beginning at the fold, for a distance of 1 inch in order to leave a tunnel opening to insert the foam bar.

6. Turn the ruffle right side out. Align the long raw edges and baste together. A tunnel will form because the back of the ruffle is shorter than the front (6a), which has extra length to accommodate the bar (6b).

7. Mark the ribbon with the finished bag length (top edge). Add the ribbon to the seam allowance and zigzag stitch over it in the same way as you did for the bottom edge (7a). Cover the end of the bar with a plastic bag. Attach a bodkin to the end of the bar and insert into the casing (7b). Draw up the ribbon and secure the ribbon ends. Hand-stitch the casing ends, catching the foam (7c).

Prepare the top closure

8. On the short end of the lips where the zipper will extend, turn under the seam allowance (see the right edges on the photo). With right sides together, place the zipper seamline over the lip seamline, turning under the zipper ends on the zipper's open end so the edge lines up with the seamline (see the zipper edges on the left side of the photo). Baste in place.

9. With right sides together, place the facing over the zipper. Machine-sew through all layers (9a, 9b on p. 76). Fold the facing with wrong sides together, aligning the long edges and turning under the seam allowances on the short seams. Baste in place and hand-stitch the short ends (9c on p. 76).

1. Add batting and muslin.

2a. Mark ribbon ½ inch and 13 inches away.

2b. Zigzag stitch over ribbon.

2c. Draw up ribbon.

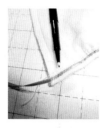

2d. Secure ribbon ends.

3. Make box pleat at center front and tucks to the left and right of center.

4a. Cut and bevel strips.

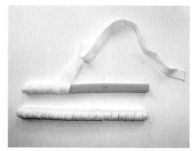

4b. Wrap with batting.

5. Fold top band ruffle over foldline.

6a. Tunnel.

6b. Extra length.

7a. Zigzag stitch over ribbon.

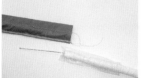

7b. Insert bar into casing.

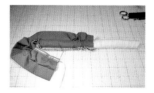

7c. Draw up ribbon to form the ruffle.

8. Line up edges with seamline.

10. With right sides together, align the ruffle with the top edge, placing it between the bag side seamlines, and secure with binder clips (10a). Center the zipper lips on top and baste in place. Machine-sew through all layers (10b).

Make a zippered pocket

11. Create a faced window for the zipper by adding a 2-inch strip of muslin on the right side of the lining, placing the edge even with the top edge of the bag. On the muslin strip, mark a window ⅜ inch high by the length of the zipper. Machine-sew through the muslin all around the window, shortening the stitch length 1 inch before reaching the corners. Cut the window down the middle, making two angle cuts at the corners. Push the muslin strip through the window to the back.

12. Place the zipper behind the window, and machine-stitch in place close to the window edge. For the pocket, cut a rectangle 1 inch wider than the window and twice as high as the pocket. Place the pocket right side over the zipper's wrong side, aligning the pocket's short end with the lower edge of the zipper tape. Sew in place (do not catch the lining in the stitching). Fold the pocket up toward the other side of the zipper tape, aligning the edges, and sew. Finish the pocket by sewing the side seams. (For more detail, see "Fold-Over Frame Bag," p. 42, steps 13–15.)

Add the lining

13. With right sides together, sew the top edge of the lining to the top edge of the bag. Repeat with the other edge. Push all the seam allowances toward the lining and, from the right side, edgestitch through the seam allowances, keeping the bag free.

14. With right sides together, sew the seam on the lining's bottom edge, leaving an opening for turning right side out. With the right sides together, pin the lining to the bag along the side edges and sew (14a, 14b). Turn the bag right side out through the bottom opening in the lining and close up the opening (14c).

Prepare and sew the gusset

15. With right sides together, sew the gusset top edge and sides, leaving an opening for turning (15a). Turn right side out. Hand-baste the gusset to the bag (15b, 15c). From the right side, machine-sew the gusset to the bag close to the edges.

Reattach the zipper slider

16. Insert the zipper slider (16a, 16b). Finish the tail end of the zipper with a scrap of fabric (16c).

9a. Machine-sew through layers (front side).

9b. Machine-sew through layers (wrong side).

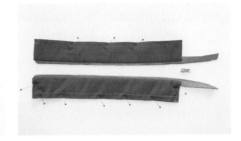

9c. Hand-stitch short ends.

10a. Align and secure ruffle with top edge.   **10b.** Center zipper and baste.

11. Cut window down the middle.

13. Sew top edge of lining to top edge of bag.

14a. Sew seam on lining bottom edge, then pin side seams.

14b. Sew bag along side seams.

14c. Turn inside out.

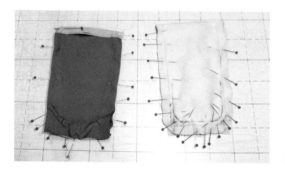

15a. Sew gusset top and edges.

15b. Hand-baste gusset to bag.

15c. Hand-baste gusset to bag (close-up).

16a. Insert zipper slider (side view).

16b. Insert zipper slider (top view).

16c. Finish tail end of zipper.

Dimensions: 11¹¹⁄₁₂ inches wide by
8 inches high by 1⅝ inches deep

Seam allowance: ⅜ inch,
unless otherwise noted

Fibers: Stingray skin and
Mirrabella pearlized lambskin

BEGINNER

Stingray Zip-Top Wristlet Clutch

TOOLS AND MATERIALS

Basic Tool Kit (p. 12)
Pattern (p. 178)
One stingray skin large enough to cut
a 6-inch by 8-inch piece
3 square feet leather or ¾ yard fabric
½ yard lining
1 yard medium curb chain
½ yard Craft-Fuse
1¼ yards of ⅛-inch ribbon
9-inch invisible zipper
Size 16 jeans needle
Size 16 leather needle
Twin needle
13½ inches of zipper tape,
#5 metal teeth
#5 zipper slider with hook
Dye (optional)
Top and bottom zipper stoppers
Two ⅝-inch twist strap rings
Closed solid ring
Decorative charm
12-inch silver flat chain
1 swivel hook

TEMPLATE

Window insert, cut one,
6 inch by 8 inch (stingray skin)

THIS LAMBSKIN maxi wristlet clutch is designed with a simple window to showcase the natural beauty of a stingray skin, which has been dyed and printed with a tiger pattern. All stingray skins have a distinctive oval-shaped mark on the spine that will not take dye pigment. No two marks are ever alike. The surface texture is granular and feels like zillions of tightly packed glass beads. The shape of the beads is symmetrical on either side of the spine, and they vary in size, with the coarsest along the spine and becoming very fine toward the side edges.

The Stingray Zip-Top Wristlet Clutch requires a little more time than the other bags, particularly when you sew the stingray skin to the window. The larger the skin, the denser the bumps, which are difficult for most sewing machine needles to pierce. The skin I use is on the smaller side, roughly 8 inches by 17 inches, which most conventional machines will be able to handle. If you encounter areas where the needle is struggling to pierce the skin, hand-walk a few stitches.

Embellish the bag front

1. Once you establish the dimensions for the stingray insert, you can plan the bag size accordingly (1a). The insert for the bag pictured here was cut 6 inches by 8 inches for a 5½-inch by 7½-inch window. On the back of the insert, mark the center points at the top and bottom edges (1b).

   NOTE When stingray is cut, the little bumps can emit glasslike chards, so wipe down your cutting surface and tool with a damp cloth to remove residual residue. The skin will also dull your blade or scissors, so you may want to use an older tool.

2. To cut a smooth continuous curve at the window corners, use the rotary cutter and penny as a guide. On the back of the window, draw a placement guideline ¼ inch above the window opening. Mark the center points at the top and bottom edges. Use easy-release tape to align the top edge of the insert with the placement guideline, matching centers at both the top and the bottom of the window (2a). Place additional tape in front, testing first to ensure the color does not lift off either material (2b).

3. Use the jeans needle (when using a leather needle, the glasslike beads and stiff material will saw the thread), two threads through the needle, and a stitch length of 8 stitches per inch to stitch all around the window. Go slowly, as you might encounter some of the beads, which could cause the needle to break. You might want to hand-walk a

few stitches around the corners so you can keep a consistent width between the stitching line and the cut edge. Remove the tape as you sew, and as you come around the corners, be sure to remove it from underneath so you don't stitch through it.

4. Frame the window with a section of curb chain. Begin with a length longer than needed and couch the chain to the edge of the window using a backstitch. Come out of the leather through an existing hole and through a link in the chain, take a backstitch going over a link, and go back down into another hole in the stitching line. Continue all the way around to where you started. Cut the chain. For an uninterrupted line, use needle-nose pliers to open the last link, connect it with the first, and close it up.

Prepare the zipper

5. Dye a section of zipper tape. Let it dry overnight, then set the color with an iron. Use side-cutting pliers to remove some of the zipper teeth (see "Security Pouch," p. 28, for instructions). Use a utility lighter to carefully sear the cut edges. Add the stoppers on the sides that will become the open end (5a, 5b). For the top stoppers, crimping pliers are ideal (5c).

Make the bag

6. Place the zipper facedown on the right side of the bag. Pay attention to the teeth orientation and be sure to align the long edges. Place the top end of the zipper at the ⅜-inch seamline, letting the bottom end extend 2 inches beyond the seamline. Using a ⁵⁄₁₆-inch seam allowance, sew the zipper to the bag, starting and stopping at the seamlines. Pull the threads to the back and tie (6a, 6b).

7. With right sides together, use binder clips to secure the gusset to the bag. Sew the seam in a continuous line, beginning and ending the stitching ¾ inch from the top cut edge (⅜ inch from the seamline).

1a. Determine dimensions for insert.

1b. Mark center points and cut insert.

2a. Use tape to align insert.

2b. Add tape to front.

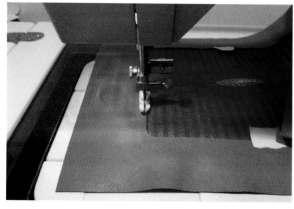
3. Stitch around window.

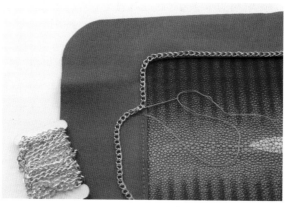
4. Frame window with curb chain.

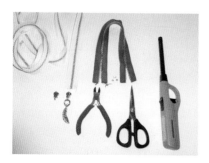
5a. and **5b.** Tools for preparing zipper.

5c. Use crimping pliers on top stoppers.

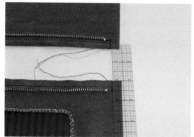
6a. Sew zipper to bag.

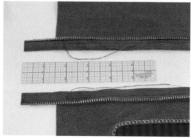
6b. Pull threads to back and tie.

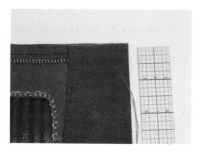
7. Sew the seam.

Stretch the gusset slightly as you go around the bottom corners and, if you need to, make very shallow clips (¹⁄₁₆ inch) on the gusset along the seamline just in the vicinity of the curve.

8. Use a mallet to pound and flatten the seams. Around tight areas that cannot lay flat, place a shaped hard object, like a rock, behind the leather. Small pieces of hardwood are good for the straighter edges (8a). Use binder clips to secure the other side of the gusset to the bag (8b). Sew the seam, starting and stopping ¾ inch from the top cut edge. Flatten the seamline in the same way. Pull all threads to the back and tie to secure.

9. From the stingray scraps, cut two strips for the wrist strap anchors. One will be placed on the bag gusset and the other at the zipper end. You will want a snug fit on the twist strap rings and at the same time be able to cover the zipper tape edges. The width on the twist strap ring is ⅝ inch and the zipper tape is 1⅛ inches, so cut the strips at ¾ inch by 2 inches for the anchor and 1¼ inches by 2⅛ inches for the zipper tail. Fold the bigger strip in half and round off the corners near the fold (trim ¼ inch at each corner) so that when you open it, it is an hourglass shape with a center width of ¾ inch. Fold it in half again, aligning the cut edges. Use the hand-sewing punch to precut the stitching holes around the three sides, going through both layers at the same time. Use a permanent marker to color all the cut edges.

10. Insert the smaller strap anchor into a twist strap ring and place it on the bag gusset, offsetting the edges slightly to reduce bulk and eliminate the need for trimming. Be sure to add it to the gusset that has the zipper opening, not the tail. Sew the anchor ⅜ inch from the bag's cut edge, secure it with a couple of rows of stitching, pull the threads to the back, and tie.

11. Beginning with the gusset, add ⅜-inch double-face tape across the upper edge on the wrong side. Peel the paper, fold down the edge ¾ inch, and adhere in place. Add double-face tape to the seam allowances on the side of the bag (11a). Peel the paper and fold the seam allowances toward the bag (11b). Repeat the folding on the other end of the gusset. Add double-face tape to the seam allowances at the top edge. Peel the paper and fold the zipper edges down toward the bag (11c).

12. From the right side, topstitch all around the top edge of the bag, starting at one end of the zipper. Use a size 16 leather needle, two threads through the needle, and a stitch length of 8 stitches/inch to topstitch ⅛ inch away from the fold (12a). When you come around the corners where the thickness is uneven, use a Hump Jumper (12b). This is one of those areas where it's a good idea to hand-walk the stitches.

13. Continue around the upper edge on the second side of the bag. With a Hump Jumper behind the foot, it is as if you had been sewing along a straight edge the entire time (13a). Return to the point where you started to finish the topstitching (13b). Leave long thread tails. Pull all the thread tails to the back and tie off (13c).

Make the lining

14. Use Craft-Fuse as interfacing for the fabric yardage (14a). Place all the lining pattern pieces on the fabric and cut out. Cut a lining divider, then fold it in half and press the edge. Open the divider, and on the back, mark a centered zipper window, ¼ inch by 8 inches, 1 inch down from the fold you just pressed. Staystitch all around the window. Add Fray Check at the corner edges, let dry, and then cut through the middle. Press back the edges, rolling the staystitching line to the back (14b). Place the zipper behind the window, baste it, and from the top edgestitch around the window to secure it. (Although ¼ inch is a fairly narrow width, by the time you roll the staystitched edge to the wrong side, the window will become ⅜ inch.)

8a. Pound and flatten seams.

8b. Use binder clips to secure other side of gusset.

9. Create wrist anchors.

10. Sew anchor to bag.

11a. Fold down gusset upper edge.

11b. Fold side seam allowances toward bag.

11c. Fold top seam allowances toward bag.

12a. Topstitch ⅛ inch from fold.

12b. Hump Jumper.

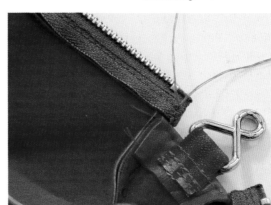

13c. Pull thread tails to back and tie off.

13a. Hump Jumper behind foot.

13b. Return to starting point.

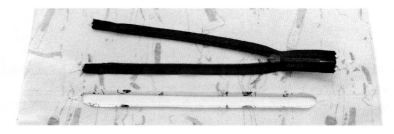

14a. Interface lining fabric.

14b. Press back window edges.

15. Place a strip of ribbon at each edge of the window and sew, using a twin needle that is slightly narrower than the ribbon. If you don't have a twin needle, use a regular one, and sew one edge at a time—you do not want to sew down the middle and take away from the ribbon.

16. Add another row of ribbon next to the fold you pressed earlier and sew. Having the darker edge will make it easier to spot the divider.

17. To form the pocket on the divider, simply fold it in half so that all the raw edges meet (17a). The inside of the pocket will show the interfaced fabric. You can add a floating pocket at this stage, if desired. For the pocket, cut a 9-inch-wide by 11-inch-high rectangle. (See steps 9–15 of "Fold-Over Frame Bag," p. 42, for further instructions.) The divider pocket is ready to be added to one wall of the lining (17b). Place the divider on a lining wall, aligning the bottom and side edges. The top edge of the divider will be $7/8$ inch from the top seamline. Baste the layers together.

18. Staystitch the lining gusset edge $1/16$ inch into the seam allowance, starting 6 inches down from the top cut edge, and stitch for a length of $4\frac{1}{2}$ inches. Repeat on the other three edges. Clip to the stay-stitching line. Pin the gusset to one side of the lining.

19. Stitch the gusset to the lining in one continuous seam, starting and stopping $3/4$ inch from the top cut edge. Secure the threads. Attach the other side of the lining to the gusset in the same way. Press the

seam allowances as sewn to set the stitching. Press back the $3/8$-inch seam allowances at the top edge, and on the gusset press back $3/4$ inch.

Add the lining

20. With wrong sides facing, clip the gussets together along one edge using binder clips, and sew within the seam allowance to secure (20a). Turn the bag right side out, pin the lining to the upper edge, and hand-sew the lining to the zipper edge (20b).

21. The slider has an open hook that is used for adding a zipper pull. Create the pull using a closed solid ring, a link from the wrist chain, and a decorative charm. Combine the three elements and add to the hook on the slider. Use pliers to close up the hook (21a). Add the slider to the zipper. At the zipper tail, attach the metal stopper, using pliers to bend the prongs (21b).

Make the wrist chain

22. Insert one end of the wrist chain into the small eye on the twist strap ring. Use two needle-nose pliers to open up the last link on the chain and hook it on the chain slightly above, forming a small loop. Close up the link to secure the loop. Insert the hourglass tab through the twist strap ring and on the wrong side add strips of $3/8$-inch double-face tape. Peel the paper and, with the zipper tail sandwiched in between, glue the tab in place.

NOTE To open a link without weakening the joint, use a push–pull motion rather than a sideways move. With a plier in one hand, hold a side of the link; with another plier in the other hand, hold the other side of the link. With the right hand push the link away from you while at the same time with the left hand pull the link toward you. To close it, reverse the direction. If you are left-handed, push and pull with the left and right, respectively.

23. Hand-stitch the tab at the zipper tail, going through the holes cut earlier. On the other end of the chain, using two pliers, open the last link, add the swivel hook, and close up the link.

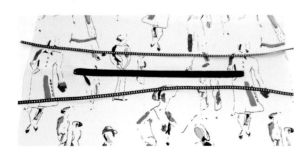

15. Sew ribbon at edge of window.

16. Add another row of ribbon.   **17a. Fold divider.**

17b. Add divider to wall of lining. Baste layers.

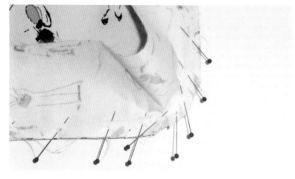

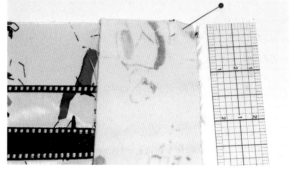

18. Pin gusset to one side of lining.

19. On gusset press back ¾ inch.

20a. Clip and sew gussets along one edge.

20b. Pin lining to upper edge.

21a. Create zipper pull and close up with pliers.

21b. Add slider to zipper.

22. Make wrist chain.

23. Add swivel hook and close up link.

INTERMEDIATE
BAGS

MAKING A REVERSIBLE LEATHER BAG can be a challenge because skins generally have an unfinished back. The solution is to finish these materials—suede fibers, for example, take well to paint. A Teflon foot comes in very handy when sewing with suede, and it's a good idea to have a variety of shapes on hand. Styles include zipper, straight stitch, and zigzag. Depending on style, these feet have different toe widths, which are useful to use as sewing guides. They are available in ⅛-inch, ¼-inch, and 5/16-inch sizes. Some styles have more clearance between the foot and the feed dogs, which is ideal for the various thicknesses a bag will have.

Dimensions: 20 inches wide by 12 inches high by 6 inches deep

Seam allowances: leather bag: ³⁄₁₆ inch at the side seams and
½ inch on the underlap; cloth bag: ⅝ inch at the top edge and
½ inch on the sides and bottom; ⅜ inch elsewhere, unless
otherwise noted

Fibers: Double-face leather and iridescent taffeta

INTERMEDIATE

Tiffany-Inspired Reversible Tote

TOOLS AND MATERIALS

Basic Tool Kit (p. 12)

Pattern (p. 180)

¾ yard fabric or 7 square feet leather

½ yard fabric (for inner bag)

Interfacing

Size 14 leather needle

24 inches of 1¼-inch-wide
zipper tape, #5 metal teeth

Two #5 sliders

Two ¾-inch anorak snaps and
setting tool

Two 1-inch spring gate O-rings

Leather hand-sewing needle

White marking pen

Clear grid ruler with
metal cutting edge

TEMPLATES

Bag straps, cut one,
4½ inch by 28 inch (leather)

Removable pouch strap, cut one,
(1½ inch by 26 inch (leather)

THIS BAG GIVES YOU two looks in one. One side of this reversible tote is distressed, while the other is flawlessly smooth suede. The detachable pouch keeps the suede side clean, and the T-shaped bottom has a lapped base and wrapped box corners. Razor-cut straps clamp onto the bag, and zipper edges on the pouch opening are totally enclosed within the seam allowance. Spring gate O-rings connect the strap to the appliquéd loops on the bag; this type of ring has a hinge that opens, so you can add it after the straps are attached. A Clover™ white marking pen is perfect for marking dark leather because it shows up nicely and wipes off easily.

Make the main bag bottom

1. Use a white marking pen to draw the placement line on the bottom edges of the bag (1a). On both the bag and the base edges, draw small perpendicular lines within the seam allowance to indicate the center points and the sides of the bag. This is where the stitching lines will begin and end (the colored pen in the photo points to the stopping points) (1b).

2. Place small pieces of ¼-inch double-face tape on the bag's underlap. Peel the paper and lap the base over the bag, matching the center and sides. Topstitch close to the cut edge, through both layers, starting at the side mark. Sew to the other side of the bag, turn the corner, and sew ¼ inch away from the first line of stitching to where you started. Pull the threads to the wrong side and tie them. Thread a needle with the tails and bury them between the layers within the seam allowances.

Set the snaps

3. Cut two 1½-inch by 3½-inch leather strips and two 1-inch by 2¾-inch strips of interfacing. The interfacing reinforces the area behind the snap. Use the foam brush to spread a coating of leathercraft cement on the back of the leather, wait a few minutes until it becomes cloudy and tacky, and then center the interfacing, add another dab of cement, and fold the strip in half.

4. On each strip, mark the snap placement ⅞ inch from the fold and ¾ inch from the sides, and use a hand-sewing leather punch to pierce the hole for the prong on the socket cap. Using an anorak snap-setting toolkit, set the snap following the manufacturer's instructions. Trim around the three sides to 1½ inches wide by 1¼ inches high, keeping the fold intact. Round off the corners. This will give you a ¼-inch border around the snap (4a). (The 1½-inch-wide measurement is the distance between the fold and the tip edge of the tab.) Align the folded edge on the tab with the cut edge of the bag and temporarily secure with a binder clip. Do not baste, which will leave a visible line of extra stitching (4b).

Sew the bag sides

5. Align the side edges and sew together ³/₁₆ inch away from the cut edge, leaving long thread tails at the top edge. Thread a needle with the tails and take several stitches over the top edge, going into the same stitching hole each time. Embroider with a buttonhole stitch to bind the overcasting threads. At the other end of the seam, tie the threads and bury them.

Sew the bottom corners

6. Matching the side seams with the center bottom, wrap the base seam allowance around the sides of the bag to enclose the cut edges. Use binder clips to hold the folded edge for sewing. Stitch close to the base cut edge, following the curve shape, and stitch again ¼ inch away, echoing the first line of stitching. Sew the other corner the same way.

7. Pull the thread tails toward the bottom on the bag's right side. Thread them on a needle and take a stitch between the leather layers, exiting at an existing hole. The easiest way to stitch is with a hand-sewing leather needle, as the knife-edge point glides easily through the leather. The downside is that when the needle accidentally slips, the prick hurts so much more than a regular needle. Use a thimble to prevent injury.

Make and attach the straps

8. Cut a 4½-inch by 28-inch leather rectangle. Use a foam brush to spread a coating of leathercraft

1a. Draw seam lines.

1b. Draw perpendicular lines.

2. Double-face tape.

3. Leathercraft cement.

4a. Set the socket part of the snap.

4b. Align edges.

5. Sew bag sides.

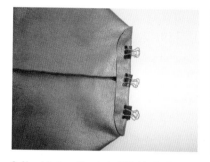
6. Use binder clips to hold folded edge.

7. Hand-stitch with thimble.

9. Prepare handles with double-face tape.

cement to the back, except the last 4 inches at each end. Wait a few minutes until it becomes cloudy and tacky, then fold the rectangle in half length-wise. Use the mallet to flatten out the rectangle, pounding over a hard surface to embed the glue and eliminate any air bubbles. Let the glue dry. Use the clear grid ruler with metal edge and rotary cutter to just barely cut off the folded edge. Use the grid lines on the ruler to cut two 1-inch-wide straps. Lift up the loose edge at the strap ends and center a strip of ¼-inch double-face tape on the wrong side. Do this on all eight edges.

9. On the bag's wrong side, mark the handle placement. Working with one layer of the strap at a time, peel the paper off the back section of the strap and tape it to the bag's wrong side. From the bag's right side

run your fingers over the tape until it is secure and you feel the ridge of the strap edges underneath. Peel the paper off the front section of the strap and carefully lay the strap on the right side of the bag, directly on top of the strap that is underneath, feeling for the ridge. Add the other end of the strap the same way. Repeat with the second strap. In the photo (on p. 91), the strap is not yet attached and not all the double-face tape has been added.

10. Sew the strap to the bag in one continuous line of stitching. Start at one corner, go all the way around to the other end of the strap, and come back to where you began. Attach the second strap to the other side of the bag in the same manner. Pull all the thread tails to the side of the bag that will be least conspicuous. Tie a tiny knot, thread a needle, and bury the threads between the strap and the bag.

Make the cloth bag insert

11. The zipper has a pretty metallic zipper tape, which is wider than normal at $1\frac{1}{4}$ inches and thus requires a $\frac{7}{8}$-inch-high window. This will give you a $\frac{3}{16}$-inch underlap on each side of the zipper tape.

Prepare the zipper for the top edge and patch pocket

12. Cut the zipper at 14 inches, remove the slider, and use side-cutting pliers to snip $\frac{3}{8}$ inch of teeth at the cut end. Use a utility lighter to carefully sear the cut edges. Reattach the slider. Close up the zipper ends, butting the edges and hand-stitching together. (The remaining zipper will be used for the patch pocket, so prepare the edges in the same way.) Cut $\frac{3}{4}$-inch by $1\frac{1}{4}$-inch leather strips to bind the zipper ends (12a). For zipper ends bound with leather, wrap the strip around each edge and sew (12b).

13. On a $6\frac{1}{4}$-inch by $10\frac{1}{2}$-inch rectangle, use the arc from a $1\frac{1}{4}$-inch circle to round off the corners. At $\frac{3}{8}$ inch down from the top edge, mark and cut a $\frac{7}{8}$-inch by 9-inch window for the zipper. Snip off the extra zipper teeth so all the teeth fit within the window. Add $\frac{1}{8}$-inch double-face tape at the zipper edges (13a). Peel the paper and center the zipper behind the window. Topstitch all around, close to the cut edge, and topstitch again at $\frac{1}{4}$ inch away (13b, 13c). Pull all the threads to the back and secure.

Sew the patch pocket

14. Center the pocket on the bag, placing it $1\frac{1}{4}$ inches down from the top seamline. Use Glad Press'n Seal to cover the edges and secure them for topstitching. Topstitch all around, close to the cut edge, and stitch again $\frac{1}{4}$ inch away. Remove the plastic wrap.

Add the zipper

15. On the right side of the fabric, press the edge down $\frac{1}{4}$ inch. Wrap the folded edge around the zipper tape wrong side, folding it by $\frac{1}{4}$ inch and placing the zipper ends 1 inch from the bag side's cut edges. Pin the folded edge all the way across the zipper.

16. Stitch close to the fold nearest the zipper teeth, through all layers (16a). Fold the bound edge down toward the bag and, from the bag's wrong side, stitch close to the fold, farthest from the zipper teeth, through all layers (16b). The finished zipper edge, when seen from the right side of the bag, shows only one row of stitching (16c). Bind the zipper to the other edge in the same way (16d on p. 95). Pictured are the finished bound edges as seen from the bag's wrong side (16e on p. 95) and the finished bound edges as seen from the bag's right side (16f on p. 95).

10. Sew strap to bag.

11. Metallic zipper tape.

12a. Strips to bind zipper ends.

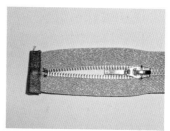

12b. Wrap leather around edge and sew.

13a. Round off corners and mark window.

13b. Sewn zipper (right side).

13c. Sewn zipper (wrong side).

14. Cover pocket with Glad Press'n Seal.

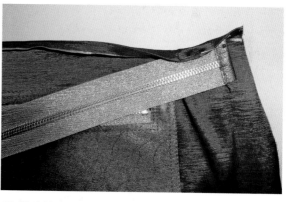

15. Pin folded edge across zipper.

16a. Stitch close to fold nearest zipper teeth.

16b. Stitch close to fold farthest from zipper teeth.

16c. Finished zipper edge.

Sew the side seams and bottom corners

17. With right sides together, pin the side edges and sew using a $3/16$-inch seam allowance. Press the seam as sewn to set the stitching. Turn the bag wrong side out and first press the seam allowances to one side of the bag, then fold the edges together and press. Stitch the seam at $1/4$ inch to enclose the raw edges. Press the seam as sewn, turn the bag right side out, and press the seam allowances to one side.

18. With right sides together, align the cut edges at the bottom corner, matching the side seam with the center bottom. Sew using a $3/16$-inch seam allowance. Repeat with the other corner. Press the seams as sewn to set the stitching, turn the bag wrong side out, and finish sewing the seam at $1/4$ inch to enclose the raw edges.

Add spring gate O-rings

19. Cut two $1\frac{1}{2}$-inch by 4-inch rectangles. Use leathercraft cement, remembering to let it get cloudy and tacky, to glue the rectangles together with wrong sides facing, offsetting the short ends $1/4$ inch so that when the loop is formed the joint seam will be staggered. Use the clear ruler and rotary cutter to make a clean edge cut on one of the long edges. From that edge, cut both strips, each $5/8$ inch wide. Add cement on the offset ends' wrong sides and overlap to form the loop. Fold the loop so the joint is $1/2$ inch from the fold. On the top of the loop, use the white marking pen to draw two stitching guidelines at $1/4$ inch and $1\frac{1}{4}$ inches from the fold, respectively. For easier sewing, add the spring gate O-rings after the loops have been sewn to the bag.

20. On the bag's wrong side, add a $7/8$-inch by 2-inch patch to reinforce the area behind the loop, centering it over the side seam and placing the top edge 1 inch down from the finished edge. Use small pieces of $1/4$-inch double-face tape to hold it in place. Note

that this is from the leftover strip from cutting the window for the zipper pocket.

21. Attach the loops on each side of the bag, centering each one over the side seam and placing the bottom fold 3 inches down from the top finished edge. Sew each loop around the side edges and over the drawn guidelines. Use a Hump Jumper for even feeding (21a). Pull the threads to the back, thread them on a needle, and bury between the leather (21b).

22. Use a $3/4$-inch circle cut from the leather to reinforce the snap placement on the bag. With the hand-sewing leather punch, pierce a hole for the prong on the stud part of the snap on both the bag and the leather disk. On the bag, cut the hole $3/4$ inch down from the top and side edge. Using the tool in the kit, set the stud, following the manufacturer's instructions.

Make the strap for the detachable bag

23. Cut a $1\frac{1}{2}$-inch by 26-inch rectangle. Use the foam brush to add a coating of leathercraft cement to the back. Wait until the glue becomes tacky, then fold the rectangle in half lengthwise. Use the mallet to flatten out the rectangle, pounding over a hard surface to embed the glue and eliminate any air bubbles. Let the glue dry. Use the clear ruler and rotary cutter to just barely cut off the folded edge. Use the ruler's grid lines to cut the strap to $5/8$ inch wide. Topstitch all around the edge of the strap. Pull all the threads to what will become the back, and tie them together. Thread a needle and take a stitch between the layers. When you exit the leather, tug on the threads to bury the knot, then cut off the excess thread. At each end fold back $1\frac{3}{8}$ inches to form the loop for the spring gate O-ring and to secure; stitch across the strap at $5/8$ inch and then $1\frac{1}{4}$ inches from the fold. Insert the rings into the strap loops and connect the strap to the loops on the bag sides.

16d. Bind zipper to other edge.

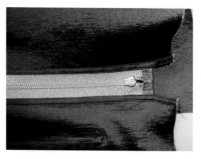

16e. Bound edges (wrong side).

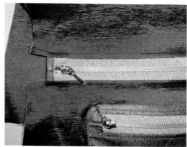

16f. Bound edges (right side).

17. Sew side seams.

19. Loops for the spring gate O-rings.

20. Add patch behind loop.

21a. Use Hump Jumper to feed loop.
21b. Bury threads.

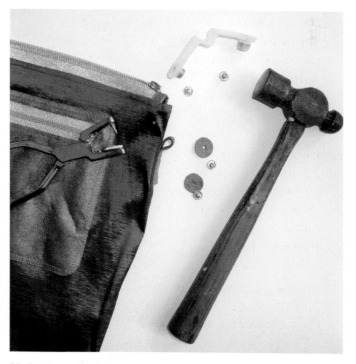

22. Set the stud part of the snap.

Dimensions: 13½ inches wide by
6 inches high by 3½ inches deep

Seam allowance: ⅜ inch,
unless otherwise noted

Fiber: Upholstery leather

INTERMEDIATE

Studded Barrel Bag

TOOLS AND MATERIALS

Basic Tool Kit (p. 12)

Pattern (p. 182)

2 square feet leather for bag or ¼ yard fabric

3 square feet contrast leather or
1 yard fabric

⅝ yard lining

¼ yard muslin

¼ yard heavyweight interfacing

13½ inches of white zipper tape, #4 metal teeth

#4 zipper slider

9-inch zipper

Paint for leather (Tandy Eco-Flo Hi-
Lite in Silver Frost shown) and zipper (Pēbēo
Setacolor opaque shown)

³⁄₁₆-inch nylon pressing bar

Curved hair clips

Snap setter with pearl adapter

Size 18 pearl snaps

Scrap of grip shelf liner

Flexible kitchen chopping mat

Silver square-cast beads

⅛-inch one-part eyelets

6 inches of ⅞-inch grosgrain ribbon

1-inch decorative buckle

TEMPLATES

Contrast leather strap, cut one ,
2½ inch by 28½ inch

Leather contrast strap for buckle end, cut one,
1¼ inches by 6 inches

Zipper pocket, cut one,
10½ inch by 12 inch
(includes ⅜-inch seam allowance)

Patch pocket, cut one,
15 inch by 6 inch
(includes ⅜-inch seam allowance)

THIS CHEERFUL bag will liven up any outfit or outing. The circle appliqués are attached to pearl snaps that pull apart, so you can remove and rearrange them in whatever color scheme suits your mood. The bag has a hobo profile that resembles a squished barrel. The seams are not linear, so it is important to keep all the pieces oriented properly and to avoid mixing them up. When you are cutting, be sure to mark the top edge on each section. Silver frost paint is used on the zipper tape, exposed edges, and the backs of the circles. The adjustable shoulder strap is just long enough that when fully extended you can sling it across your back, quiver-style. The fringed tip is not just for decoration; it reduces the bulk that a turned-back edge would create and is a way of dealing with an average-looking tip.

97

Prepare exposed cut edges

1. Use a stainless-steel edge paddle to dab paint along all the exposed cut edges, extending slightly to the back so the lips on all the edges look finished. On the bag, paint the sides on the spread seams and the sides that overlap the zipper, including the short ends on the facing strips. Keep a damp rag nearby to immediately wipe off excess. You have only a few minutes before the paint begins to dry.

Assemble front and back

2. Place one bag side panel on top of a facing strip, overlapping it ⅜ inch. Stitch close to the cut edge, leaving long thread tails. Add a facing strip to the center panel, making sure it is not the same edge that will connect to the panel you just sewed. Add the remaining facing strips in the same way.

3. Baste the side panel to the center panel with a small piece of double-face tape placed just at the top edge. Remove the paper and tack just the corner edge of the center panel to the facing strip, using the nylon pressing bar as a guide for spacing.

4. Stitch the center panel to the facing, with the cut edges touching the space bar. Because you are sewing on a curve, you will need to reposition the bar as you sew the seam so the cut edges can always be touching the bar. The height on the spacing bar and on the leather edges is the same, so sewing the seam is easy because the presser foot is balanced. Sew the other panels to the facing strip in the same way. Tie the thread tails, thread them on a needle, and bury in the back. This is especially important at the top edge, which will be exposed when it is sewn to the zipper.

Make the zipper

5. Paint the zipper tape. I used Pēbēo Setacolor paint in opaque, which does not penetrate the cloth as easily as a dye, so use a stiff brush to apply. Work it into the fibers and between the teeth. Let dry overnight. To set the paint, iron the zipper tape.

6. The strap will eventually attach at the point where the zipper ends. To prevent the zipper from meeting at the strap junction, cut it shorter than the opening edge and add extension tabs. The 1-inch-wide zipper is cut at 13½ inches; cut the tabs 1⅜ inches wide by 1 inch long. The longer side on the tab is placed across the zipper. For a graded edge, cut it wider than the zipper ends. Insert the zipper slider (6a). Overlay a tab at each end of the zipper and stitch close to the cut edge. Stitch again ¼ inch away (6b).

7. Align the zipper with the top edge of the bag, placing the zipper teeth ⅛ inch away from the cut edge. Use curved hair clips to secure the two (7a). Machine-stitch close to the cut edge. Add the other side of the bag to the zipper, but before sewing the seam, align the decorative seams across from each other. Secure each intersection with a small hand stitch, going through the existing holes (7b). Machine-sew the edge to the zipper (7c).

Embellish with snaps

8. It can be challenging to center the snap within a circle, as even a variance as slight as ¹⁄₃₂ inch is visible to the eye. It is more accurate to set the snap on a larger piece of leather and then cut out the circle. Paint enough of the leather wrong side for thirty-five 1½-inch squares. Cut the squares. On each square mark the center point.

1. Dab paint on exposed edges.

2. Leave long thread tails.

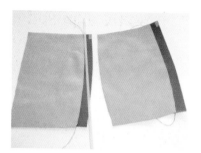

3. Nylon pressing bar.

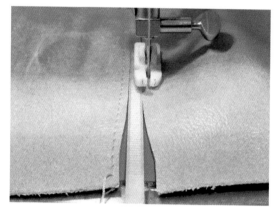

4. Stitch center panel to facing.

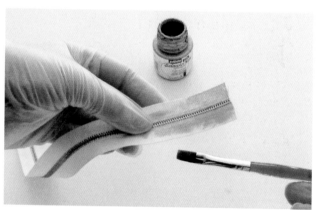

5. Paint zipper tape.

6a. Cut zipper and tabs.

6b. Stitch tabs to zipper.

7a. Secure with hair clips.

7b. Secure with hand stitch.

7c. Machine-sew edge to zipper.

8. Mark center point on squares.

9. A three-part setting tool sets a snap without the prongs shifting. The base plate has a post that locks the other two plates and an indentation that holds the prong securely. The size is specific to the size of the snap being set (other base plates are available for different sizes and styles). The middle plate has an opening in which to place the socket or stud, and the top plate locks everything and is used for striking the hammer.

10. Center a pearl snap on the square over the mark, pushing the prongs through the leather. Use the end of a tool to push down. The farther the prongs stick out of the leather, the more stable the snap will be (10a). Place the square, with the pearl snap attached, facedown on the base plate (10b). Add the middle plate and place the stud in the hole (10c). Add the top plate and strike with the hammer.

11. Add the remaining studs to the squares in the same manner. Make sure all the settings are tight by inserting a fingernail in between to see if they give. If one feels loose in any way, put it back in the tool and hammer. Go easy, though; you don't want to crack the pearl.

Cut the circles

12. Place a 1⅜-inch circle template on top of the square, centering the snap. For accuracy, measure the distance at the vertical and horizontal points marked on the template to be sure they are equidistant. Use a fine-tip pen that does not bleed to lightly trace the circle.

13. To replicate a punched hole with flush edges, keep the blades perpendicular to the cut edge as you are cutting. Cut just inside the traced line so you don't leave any pen marks. As you are cutting, butt your index finger up against the side of the bottom blade to stabilize the scissors and cut deep within the blades. Keep the scissors very still and rotate the circle as you cut.

14. Arrange the circles with the snaps as you see fit, overlapping some more than others (14a). Place tissue paper over the cluster and mark the snap center points. Use a Crop-A-Dile II to cut out the points on the stencil (14b). Place the stencil on the bag where desired. Transfer the points, marking through the stencil holes with a chalk pencil or another removable marking tool. (The socket has an open center, so permanent marks will be visible.) To mark the remaining placement points, scatter the circles and use a chalk pencil to lightly mark their placement.

Add the sockets

15. Position the prong ring on the back of the bag, then push the prongs to pierce the leather. Push down on the leather so the prongs protrude as much as possible. The farther they stick out, the tighter the setting will be. Add all the sockets to the bag, including on the base. Check that all settings are tight. If you plan on rearranging the snaps, stabilize them with a 1-inch square of interfacing on the back.

16. The maximum reach on the snap-setting tool is 2¾ inches from the edge, but you can use it beyond this range if you remove the locking post. You will need to be extra-careful because the plates are not as secure and can move. To prevent shifting, use scraps of grip shelf liner between the plates.

Make the base

17. Add a pillowcaselike pocket for the plastic insert. Cut a piece of muslin the same size as the base, position it on the wrong side, and baste the long edges with a ¼-inch seam allowance (17a). With right sides together, sew the base to one side of the bag, using binder clips to hold the edges together (17b).

9. Top, middle, and base plates.

10a. Prongs sticking out.

10b. Place square on base plate.

10c. Place stud in hole.

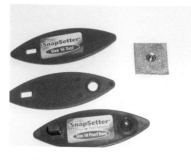

11. Add remaining studs to squares.

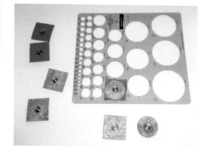

12. Circle template.

13. Cut circles.

14a. Arrange circles with snaps.

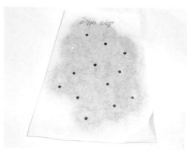

14b. Cut out points with Crop-A-Dile II.

15. Pierce leather.

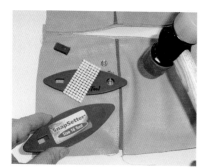

16. Shelf liner.

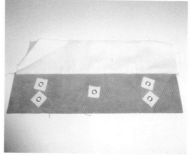

17a. Baste muslin.

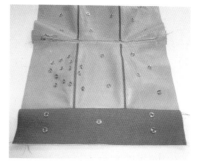

17b. Sew base to side of bag.

18. Push all the seam allowances away from the bag toward the base, and from the right side edgestitch close to the fold through all layers (18a). With right sides together, and using binder clips to hold the edges, sew the base to the other side of the bag (18b). Turn all the seam allowances toward the base, and from the right side edgestitch close to the fold through all layers (18c). Round off all the corners of the plastic insert, so they do not cut through the leather. Insert the plastic between the leather and muslin (18d). (The plastic insert is cut without seam allowances.)

Make the strap

19. The depth on the fringe is 3 inches, so paint the strap end a distance of 4 inches. Draw a line down the center of the strap (19a). Place the strap end under a slotted ruler and cut up to the 3-inch mark, using the ¼-inch cutting slots (19b). Use the foam brush to spread leathercraft cement over the entire strap except for the fringe end (19c). Let the glue become cloudy and tacky (19d). Fold the strap edges so they meet at the center line (19e). Use the mallet to flatten out the bumps, pounding on a hard surface, and let dry.

20. Topstitch the strap close to the folded edge, starting at the end with the raw edge. Stitch to the fringed end, across it to the other edge, and back to where you started. Stitch again, using the presser foot width as stitching guide. Sew toward the fringe, then go across it, stitching in the same holes, and

down on the other side using the presser foot width as your stitching guide. Use the stainless-steel edge paddle to paint the cut edges on the fringe. Let dry. Insert a metal square bead, and tie a knot.

21. Use a Crop-A-Dile II to punch ⅛-inch holes for the eyelets, centering them on the strap. Set the eyelets with the Crop-A-Dile II (21a). The strap at the buckle end is made with one leather layer and reinforced with a grosgrain ribbon. It is cut 1¼ inches wide by 6 inches long; the ⅞-inch-wide ribbon is cut the same length. Paint the leather's cut edges on the long sides, going over the edge into the back about ¼ inch (21b).

22. Use a foam brush to cover the strap with leather-craft cement (22a). Wait a few minutes until it becomes cloudy and tacky and place the ribbon over the glue (22b). Let the glue dry. Pierce the hole for the buckle prong ¼ inch away from the center so when the strap is folded the short edges are offset by ¼ inch. (The center is found by folding the strap in half with the short ends meeting (22c).) Insert the buckle by pushing the prong through the hole you just pierced (22d), and sew layers together as far as possible. Sew the strap end to one side of the bag and the buckle end to the other side (22e).

Add the oval sides

23. To create a pocket for the plastic insert, cut two additional ovals from muslin. Add the muslin to each oval and baste all around, using a ¼-inch seam allowance (23a on p. 105). Use binder clips to

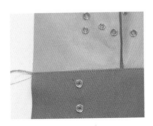
18a. Edgestitch through all layers.

18b. Use binder clips to secure edges.

18c. Edgestitch through all layers.

18d. Insert plastic between leather and muslin.

19a. Draw a line down center of strap.

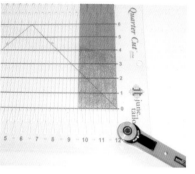

19b. Cut up to 3-inch mark.

19c. Leathercraft cement.

19d. Cloudy, tacky cement.

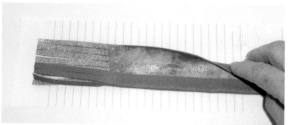

19e. Fold strap edges.

20. Add beads to fringe.

21a. Set eyelets.

21b. Paint leather cut edges.

22a. Cover strap with leather-craft cement.

22b. Place ribbon over glue.

22c. Cut prong hole.

22d. Insert buckle.

22e. Sew strap end and buckle end.

fasten the oval sides to the bag, aligning the edges and pairing with the corresponding match points (23b). Stretch the seam allowance on the bag edge slightly. If it is not enough, make tiny 1/16-inch clips along the seam allowance on the bag side. Be sure the oval is attached in the proper orientation, with the smallest end at the zipper edge. Sew with the bag side toward the feed dogs (23c).

24. Cut a slit in the muslin layer, being careful not to cut the leather (24a). Add the plastic insert, rolling it into a burritolike shape. Once the insert is between the layers, release and adjust so it lies flat against the leather. Note that the plastic inserts are cut without seam allowances (24b). Use a cat stitch to hand-sew the opening closed (24c).

Add the lining

25. The lining pieces are, from top to bottom, as follows:

   • Interfacing for facing, cut two

   • Facing, cut two

   • Oval sides, cut two

   • Bag front/back, cut one

   • Zippered pocket, cut one (10½ inches wide by 12 inches long)

   • Patch pocket, cut one (15 inches wide by 6 inches deep)

   The pocket measurements include a 3/8-inch seam allowance.

26. Sew the darts in the lining. There are four darts at the top edge (two at each end), and two shaped like fisheyes at the base. Add interfacing to the facings. With the interfacing side down, add the facings to the bag, aligning the facing's top edge with the bag's top edge. Sew the facing to the bag all around.

27. At one end of the bag add a zippered pocket. At the other end add a patch pocket that spans the width of the bag (27a). Customize the patch pocket with divided slots (for items such as a notebook, pen, or mobile phone), sewing vertical rows along the width. Reinforce the zipper ends with small leather triangles left over from cutting the circles (27b).

28. Before closing up the sides of the bag to insert the ovals, build a little bridge between the top edges to accommodate the width of the zipper. You need to add a span ½ inch across by ¾ inch in length, plus seam allowances. Cut the bridge on the fold so the edge closest to the zipper opening has a clean finish. Adding 3/8-inch seam allowances, each insert will measure 1¼ inches across by 2¼ inches in length. When folded it will measure 1¼ inches across by 1⅛ inches in length.

29. Staystitch the edges on the bag just inside the seam allowances. Clip the seam within the seam allowance. Pin the oval to the bag, aligning with the corresponding match points. Sew all around. Repeat on the other oval.

Secure the lining

30. Pin the ovals in their final position to ensure you don't end up with a pretzel for a lining. With the bag right side out, drop the lining into the bag in the finished position. Reach into the bag at the oval end and grab both the lining's and bag's seam allowances as if they were in their finished position. Use a safety pin to hold them together. Do the same on the other oval. Turn the bag wrong side out, being careful that the safety pins do not come undone. Align the ovals with their respective match points and secure with binder clips. To permanently secure, machine-stitch all around each oval within the seam allowances, removing the binder clips and safety pins as you sew.

31. Turn the bag so the lining is right side out. Pin the lining edge to the zipper and hand-sew to close the edge. Turn bag right side out.

23a. Cut and baste ovals.

23b. Use binder clips to fasten oval sides to bag.

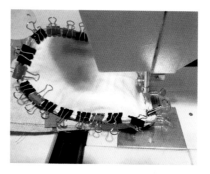

23c. Sew with bag side toward feed dogs.

24a. Cut a slit in muslin layer.

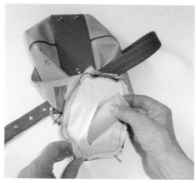

24b. Add plastic insert.

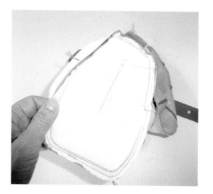

24c. Sew opening closed.

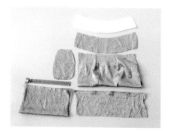

25. Lining pieces.

26. Sew darts in lining.

27a. Add patch pockets

27b. Reinforce ends.

28. Build bridge.

29. Staystitch edges.

30. Drop lining into bag.

Dimensions: 13½ inches wide by
18 inches high by 3½ inches deep

Seam allowance: Center front edge has no seam
allowance; ⅜ inch elsewhere, unless otherwise noted

Fiber: Pigskin suede

INTERMEDIATE

North–South Convertible Tote

TOOLS AND MATERIALS

Basic Tool Kit (p. 12)

Pattern (p. 185)

6 square feet suede for bag,
6½ square feet suede for details,
or 1½ yards fabric

½ yard lining and ½ yard flannel

Size $^{4.0}/_{100}$ Jeans/Denim double needle

37½ inches of zipper tape,
#6 metal teeth

Two #6 zipper sliders

1⅝ yards of ³⁄₁₆-inch ribbon

Two 1¼-inch rectangular rings

9 inches of 1-inch grosgrain ribbon

Magnetic snap

Scrap of bag stiffener

1½ yards of 1-inch horsehair

24 inches of ¼-inch wooden dowel

Two 1¼- inch swivel clasps

¾ yard fine chain

8 daisy rosettes (¼-inch
bead spacers)

2 inches of ¼-inch-wide flat chain

TEMPLATES

Detachable Strap, cut one,
3 inch by 45 inch (suede)

Patch pocket, cut one,
10 inch by 10 inch (fabric)

Pouch for zippered pocket, cut one,
9½ inch by 16 inch (fabric)

Dowel cover, cut one, 1½ inch by
13½ inch (contrasting suede)

THE SILHOUETTE of this convertible tote resembles a garment with vestlike details, such as shoulders, V neckline, and armholes. It has two grips, handles made from wooden dowels, and a supple detachable strap interfaced with horsehair to shape it without rigidity. The detachable strap conforms to the body, attaching to flanges that protrude at a 45-degree angle. The center front features an expandable gusset that zips closed for a smaller profile. The bag sews up easily. The key is detaching the slider from the zipper teeth, so the center panel is wide open, and partially sewing crossing seams, which allows you to work as flat as possible to complete the next step without being constricted.

Sew the bag

1. With right sides together, sew the two bottom darts. Use the mallet, pounding over a hard surface, to press them open. Repeat on the other three sections of the bag (1a). From the top, edgestitch on each side of the seam. For a prominent line of stitching, use two threads in the needle and lengthen the stitch to 8 stitches/inch (1b). Trim the seam allowances. Pull all threads to the back, tie, and trim the tails (1c).

2. With right sides together, partially sew the bottom seam just beyond the first dart, and open the seam. Repeat on the other section of the bag (2a). From the right side, edgestitch on each side of the seam to just before the first dart. Leave the long thread tails. Repeat on the other section of the bag (2b). Cut the zipper down to 28 inches (the remainder will be used for the pocket in the lining). Remove the zipper slider, if one is inserted, and separate the zipper. On each end, use side-cutting pliers to snip off a few teeth so ½ inch of the zipper tape is free of teeth. Place the zipper down on the topside of the wedge, aligning the edges. Sew each side ⅛ inch away from the zipper teeth (2c).

3. With the wedge wrong side down, lay one side of the bag on top of the zipper with the bag edge just covering the previous stitching line on the zipper tape. Stitch close to the bag's raw edge (3a). To ensure the bag does not end up askew, temporarily insert the slider and zip up the gusset. Attach the other side of the bag, aligning the center bottom seams. Start stitching at that point, taking care not to catch the gusset (3b). After sewing a few stitches, remove the slider and continue sewing to the top edge (3c). Finish sewing the other end.

4. Staystitch the ruffle seam edge ⅛ inch away from the cut edge, then clip the seam allowance up to the sewn edge, spacing the clips ¼ inch apart. Place the ruffles on top of the bag's edge just covering the bag's cut edge, overlapping at the bottom by ¼ inch. Beginning at the overlap, sew directly on top of the staystitching line and continue to the top edge (4a). Return to the bottom and finish sewing the ruffle on that side. Add the ruffle to the other side of the bag in the same manner, starting at the bottom edge (4b). Cover the cut edges with a decorative ribbon, and use a double needle to sew in place. To ensure you catch both edges, select a needle width slightly narrower than your ribbon (4c). Insert the zipper slider; be sure it is oriented in the proper direction.

5. Make the flange anchors for the detachable strap. Add ¼-inch double-face tape on the back of the tabs, then peel back the paper and fold the tab, bringing the edges to the center (5a). Insert a rectangular ring through the tab and fold in half, aligning the raw edges. Place the folded tab on the right side of the flange, adding it to the edge of the

1a. Press open seams.

1b. Use two threads in needle.

1c. Tie and trim tails.

2a. Sew bottom seam just beyond first dart.

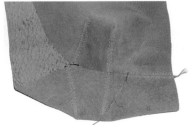

2b. Edgestitch on right side.

2c. Sew zipper to wedge.

3a. Stitch close to raw edge.

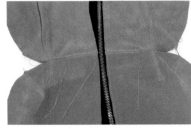

3b. To match bottom seams, insert slider and zip up gusset.

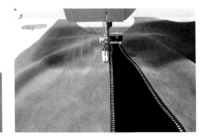

3c. Remove slider and sew to top edge.

4a. Staystitch ruffle and add to bag.

4b. Add ruffle to other side.

4c. Add decorative ribbon.

5a. Double-face tape.

5b. Fold triangle over tab and clip.

triangle with the longer side. Fold the triangle over the tab, clip (5b on p. 109), baste the seam, and turn right side out. Make the other flange anchor in the same manner.

6. Use a 4½-inch piece of grosgrain ribbon to reinforce the seamline on each side of the bag where the flanges will be sewn (6a). Clip the triangular flanges to the sides of the bag. Baste in place (6b). Finish sewing the side seams, stopping at the seamline at the top edge of the bag. Use the mallet, pounding over a hard surface, to press them open (6c).

7. Add a magnetic snap to the facing. Cut a piece of bag stiffener slightly larger than the snap. Use the metal plate and chalk pencil to mark the hole placement on suede facing and on the bag stiffener. Cut the holes for the prongs on both the stiffener and the suede. Push the snap prongs through the suede, and on the back add the stiffener and the metal plate. Use small pliers to bend the prongs toward center. Add the second part of the magnetic snap to the other facing. To protect the metal edges from cutting the bag, spread leathercraft cement on a scrap of suede and over the bent prongs, wait until the glue becomes cloudy and tacky, and secure the patch over the bent prongs. Let the glue dry.

8. With right sides together, sew one facing to one side of the bag at the upper edge (shoulderlike seams). Repeat with the other facing. Open the seams and edgestitch on each side of the seam.

9. With right sides together, sew the facing to the bag at the center (like a neckline), stopping ¾ inch from the upper edge seamline to allow for the casing. Repeat on the other side of the bag. Clip inside corners and grade the seam allowances (9a). On the sides of the bag (armholelike), use a chalk pencil to mark the intersection of the seamlines (underarmlike point). Mark the same points on the facings (9b).

10. You want the facing to be narrower than the bag so the edge will roll automatically to the back. Trim the facing (armhole) seam allowances ¹⁄₁₆ inch; so as not to change the armhole length, taper to nothing at the underarm (10a, 10b). With right sides together, sew the facings' short seams (underarm), stopping at the seamline that you marked.

11. Align the bag and facing edges and sew the seam (armhole), starting at the chalked line and stopping ¾ inch from the top edge (to allow for the casing). Repeat on the other side, sewing the armhole edges. Grade the seams. Clip all the curves just shy of the seamline. Alternate the clips on the bag and facing, so there is no void to create a valley when the curve is released. Valleys cause dimples along the edge when the edge is turned right side out.

12. Turn the facings right side out and from the right side of the bag, topstitch the necklines, stopping ¾ inch from the top edge (12a). Finish edgestitching the side seams on the bag, beginning where you left off at the bottom of the bag (don't overlap the stitching; when finished, pull threads to back and tie together) and stopping just before the seamline at the top edge of the bag (underarm). Be careful not to catch the facing (12b). Switch to a zipper foot when edgestitching around the flanges. In tight, problematic areas, it is best to hand-walk the machine stitching (12c).

13. Topstitch the armhole edges, starting ¾ inch from top edge and stopping at previous lines of stitching on the side of the bag (at the underarm). To blend the stitching lines, don't overlap the stitching; instead, pull threads to the back and tie together.

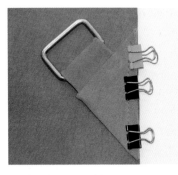
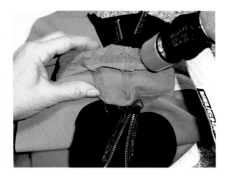

6a. Reinforce seamline with grosgrain ribbon.

6b. Clip flanges and baste.

6c. Open seam and pound it.

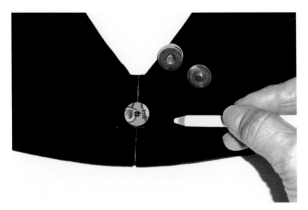
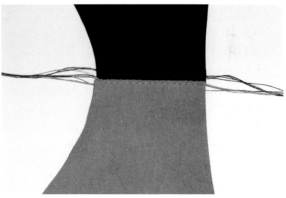

7. Add magnetic snap.

8. Sew facing to one side of bag.

9a. Grade seam allowances.

9b. Mark intersection of seamlines.

10a. Trim seam allowances.

10b. Taper at armhole.

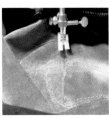

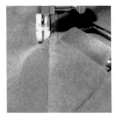

11. Sew armhole seam.

12a. Topstitch neckline.

12b. Edgestitch side seams.

12c. Hand-walk in tight areas.

13. Topstitch armhole edges.

Make the lining

14. Underline the main section of the bag with flannel. Stitch the flannel all around the edges (14a). To hold the layers together neatly when the gusset is zipped up, place two vertical rows of stitching following the same angles as the gusset, replicating the embroidery pattern found on the yardage (14b).

15. Add a patch pocket. For perfect grainlines on straight edges, it is best to tear the fabric, rather than cut it, so tear a 10-inch by 10-inch square. Stabilize the top edge with horsehair so the pocket does not collapse. Place a 1-inch strip of horsehair on the right side of the pocket at the top edge (15a). Fold the edge down so it encases the horsehair. Stitch the edge, using a decorative stitch (15b). Press under the raw edges on the sides of the pocket. Center it on one section of the lining and stitch the sides and bottom edge (15c).

16. Add a zippered pocket. This fabric frays easily and the window height is pretty narrow, so use a separate facing to stabilize the opening before sewing the zipper. On the right side, center a 3-inch by 12-inch facing over the window and stitch a $5/16$-inch-high by $8\frac{1}{2}$-inch-long rectangle. Use Fray Check on the corners, applying it just inside the window, and let it dry. Cut through the window center, up to $\frac{1}{2}$ inch from the ends, and then cut across diagonally to

each corner just shy of the stitching line (16a). Push the facing through the window and press. Place the zipper behind the window and edgestitch all around (16b). If using zipper tape, use side-cutting pliers to remove $\frac{1}{2}$ inch of zipper teeth at each end and insert the slider before sewing it to the window.

17. For the pocket pouch, cut a $9\frac{1}{2}$-inch-wide by 16-inch-long rectangle. Line up the narrower edge of the rectangle with the bottom zipper lip (17a). Use a zipper foot to sew the two edges together, keeping the facing and bag free. Push all the seam allowances away from the zipper teeth and, from the right side, understitch the pocket, keeping the bag free (17b). Bring up the other edge of the rectangle and line up with the upper zipper lip (17c). Stitch, keeping the bag free. Pin the side edges together. Sew the seams, keeping the bag free.

18. Sew the darts at the bottom corners and press to one side on each section, alternating the direction of the dart legs to distribute the bulk. With right sides facing, sew the two bag sections together along the outer edge, leaving a 6-inch opening at the bottom to turn the bag right side out. With right sides together, drop the bag into the lining, matching centers and side seams, and secure with binder clips (18a). Sew all around the top edge. Turn the bag right side out, reach in through the opening in the

14a. Stitch around flannel edges.

14b. Replicate embroidery pattern.

15a. Add horsehair to bag's top edge.

15b. Use decorative stitch.

15c. Stitch sides and bottom.

16a. Cut through window center.

16b. Place zipper and edgestitch all around.

17a. Bottom flap.

17b. Understitch pocket.

17c. Line up other edge with zipper tape.

18a. Use binder clips to secure lining to facing.

18b. Understitch lining.

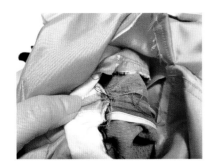

18c. Tack seam allowances to facings.

18d. Tack wedge seams.

18e. Line up darts and tack seam allowances at bottom corners.

lining, push all the seam allowances away from the facing, and understitch the lining, sewing through all the layers and taking care not to catch the bag (18b on p. 113). At the bag's side seams, tack the seam allowances to the facings (18c on p. 113). At center front, tack the wedge seams to the corresponding points on the facing (18d on p. 113). To keep the lining from shifting inside the bag, tack the seam allowances together at the bottom corners (18e on p. 113). Close up the opening in the lining.

Make the handles and strap

19. With a fine-tooth saw, cut a ¼-inch wooden dowel into two 12-inch pieces (19a). Cut a piece of suede 1½ inches by 13½ inches (the suede is cut 1½ inches longer than the dowel so you can wrap it around the ends). Apply ⅜-inch double-face tape all around the edges (19b). Peel the paper and wrap the suede around the dowel, tucking in the ends to cover the dowel edges (19c). With a chalk pencil, trace around the leaf design and cut. Trace and cut three additional leaves (19d, 19e). Apply double-face tape at the base of each leaf cluster. Peel back the paper and then wrap around each dowel end (19f, 19g). Cover the dowel end with a small plastic sandwich bag so it glides easily through the material, and insert it through two casings at the top edge of the bag. Repeat with the other handle.

20. For the strap, cut a 3-inch by 45-inch strip of suede and 46 inches of 1-inch horsehair. If the suede is not long enough to cut in one continuous length, cut the strap in three sections so the piecing seam does not sit on the shoulder. To piece the strap, overlap the edges ⅜ inch, stitch close to the cut edge, and stitch again a presser foot width away (20a). Fold the strip over the horsehair and stitch close to the cut edge. Topstitch the other edge, stitching close to the fold. Using the presser foot width as a guide, sew two additional rows, placing each one parallel and next to the previous line of stitching along the edges (20b). Attach the swivel clasps at the end of the strap, turning back each end 1½ inches. Hand-sew to secure. Wrap a length of fine chain and hand-stitch to secure (20c).

Add the decorative details

21. Add details to provide embellishment and stabilization. Reinforce the bag's side edges with a tack spanning the seamline. Decorate the tack with beads, placing a bead on each side of the seam. Bracket the joint with two additional beads on the facing (21a, 21b). For a zipper stopper, hand-tack a 1-inch length of ¼-inch-wide chain at the zipper's end on the top edge of the bag. Repeat on the other top edge (21c, 21d).

19a. Cut dowel.

19b. Double-face tape.

19c. Wrap suede around dowel.

19d. Trace leaves.

19e. Cut leaves (flip 2 for mirror images).

19f. Double-face tape.

19g. Adhere leaves to dowel ends.

20a. Piece strap.

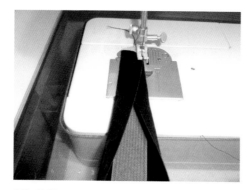

20b. Fold strap and stitch.

20c. Wrap chain and stitch.

21a. Decorate with beads (outside).

21b. Decorate with beads (inside).

21c. Hand-tack zipper on top edge.

21d. Repeat on other top edge.

Dimensions: 12 inches wide by
6½ inches high by 1¾ inches deep

Seam allowance: ½ inch, unless otherwise noted

Fibers: Croc-embossed lambskin,
lamb suede, pearlized lambskin (piping)

INTERMEDIATE

Leather and Suede Envelope Clutch

TOOLS AND MATERIALS

Basic Tool Kit (p. 12)

Pattern (p. 188)

1 leather skin, 2 square feet,
and 1 suede skin (contrast),
1½ square feet or ⅝ yard fabric and
¼ yard fabric (contrast).

⅝ yard light- to medium-weight
fabric for lining

Size 14 Microtex needle

2 flexible kitchen chopping mats or
⅝ yard craft-weight fusible
interfacing

2 yards of 3⁄32-inch cotton cable
cord for piping

Adhesive dot roller

Decorative turn-lock clasp with
screw back

Size 5 or 7 leather glover's
hand needle

T
HIS STREAMLINED envelope clutch is just big enough to carry comfortably in the crook of your arm without being too large and cumbersome. Gussets enable the bag to expand and contract as needed, so all your essentials will fit without distorting its shape. Choose a variety of materials, including real and faux leather or upholstery-weight fabrics.

117

Prepare the bag pieces

1. An ordinary flexible kitchen chopping mat between the outer fabric and lining gives just the right amount of stiffness and a firm roll to the clutch body. You can easily substitute a craft-weight fusible interfacing, such as Craft-Fuse; however, the result will not be as stiff and resilient. Piping is optional; customize your own or use purchased piping.

   NOTE Don't use pins on leather. Instead, temporarily secure the bag sections to each other with Glue Dots® or double-face tape along the edges.

2. All diagonal edges of the clutch diamond base and the front flap/upper back sections can be piped. Cut the piping for each edge. On the bag section's right side, align the piping seamline with the bag seamline. Temporarily affix the piping with Glue Dots or double-face tape. With a zipper foot, stitch the piping in place.

3. Apply the stiffener. Stick Glue Dots or double-face tape onto each bag section's wrong side, except the gussets. Finger press the stiffener pieces in place, making sure they stick to the adhesive. Fold the seam allowance on the upper back edges and diamond, base front and back edges to the wrong side over the stiffener pieces and adhere with tape or Glue

Dots. Binder clips may be necessary to hold the piped edges in place.

Assemble the bag

4. Join the bag sections. With right sides up, lap the front flap/upper back section over the upper side back sections, matching the seamlines. From the right side, edgestitch through all layers (4a). Then lap one piped edge of the base section over the side backs' lower edges, with the point overlapping the upper back's indentation (4b). Edgestitch in place. Finally, lap the remaining piped edge of the base section over the upper front section and edgestitch in place (4c).

5. Add the toggle clasp. Transfer the toggle clasp placement mark from the clutch pattern onto the base section's front point. Center the toggle plate over the marking, and press the prongs into the surface to make an impression. Use the utility knife to cut slits and insert the toggle plate's prongs from the right side. On the wrong side, apply the toggle's backing plate. Use pliers to bend the prongs inward.

6. Line the clutch body. On the lining tip end, interface and staystitch the area. With the bag exterior and lining right sides together, sew along the front

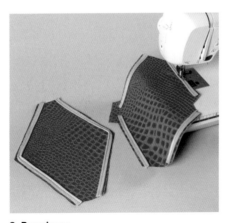

2. Bag pieces.

3. Apply stiffener to pieces.

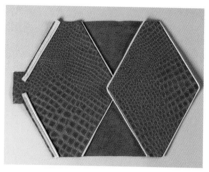

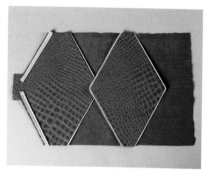

4a. Lap sections.

4b. Lay piped edge of base over side backs.

4c. Lap remaining piped edge over upper front section.

5. Add toggle clasp.

6a. Sew lining to body.

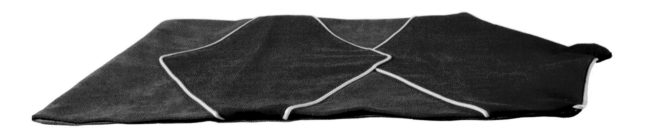

6b. Close opening's folded edges.

flap edges, one long edge, and the upper front's top edge, leaving one long edge unsewn. Clip the clasp end's inner corners (6a on p. 119). Turn the bag right side out through the opening. Fold under the opening's seam allowances; use double-face tape or Glue Dots to stick the folded edges together (6b on p. 119).

Sew and insert the gussets

7. With right sides together, sew the gusset lining to the gusset at the top edge. Open the layers and press the seam allowance toward the lining. Under-stitch the lining, securing it to the seam allowance.

8. Sew the lining and gusset darts separately. Fold each gusset section in half lengthwise, right sides together. Align the lower edges to form the darts, and stitch ½ inch from the raw edge.

FOUNDATIONS, LININGS, HARDWARE

Search for unusual materials in your home and work-space to reach beyond the traditional interfacings that are commonly used for foundations. Any material that can be cut, sewn through, and washed (if needed) can work as an interfacing. A well-thought-out lining is an extension of a beautiful external design. In the North–South Convertible Tote, the leaf embroidery inspired the dangling leaf clusters. The silver paint on the Studded Barrel Bag is reflected in the lining, and the black-and-white linen on the Cross-Body Sling Bag with Tablet Pocket is evocative of the Internet. For a cohesive look, use coordinating hardware throughout your creation—and think beyond its decorative purpose for covering up unwanted visuals or acting as stabilizers.

9. Fold the gusset lining into the gusset, right sides together, matching the dart seams. Fold the top seam allowance down, toward the dart. Use binder clips to hold all the edges together. Beginning at one top edge, sew around the gusset, stitching the lining and exterior together. Leave an opening for turning. Turn the gusset right side out, fold under the opening's edges, and close it with double-face tape or Glue Dots.

10. Temporarily adhere the gussets to the bag. Place Glue Dots along the gusset's edges on the wrong side. Align the gusset's top front edge ½ inch below the bag front's top edge, wrong sides together. Cup the bag's body around the gusset and press the edges together. Use binder clips to secure them for stitching. Baste, using a slipstitch.

11. A leather bag may not fit under a presser foot at this stage, so hand-sew the gussets in place with a glover's leather needle (be sure to wear a thimble). Take small slipstitches through both folded edges. Sew around the gusset, first in one direction, then in the other, going through the existing holes. If your bag is fabric, machine-sew the gussets in place, stitching close to the folds.

Finish with the clasp

12. Mark and cut the socket plate location. Using the clasp's bottom socket plate as a template, mark the screw holes and draw an outline of the opening for the toggle. Pierce the screw holes through the flap and lining with the Crop-a-Dile II, then use a utility knife to finish cutting the socket plate opening.

13. Install the clasp socket plates. Place the clasp's top plate on the flap's right side and the bottom plate on the flap's underside. Align the holes and screw the plates in place. If the socket plates seem loose, insert a scrap of leather or a bit of packing foam between the flap underside and the bottom plate.

7. Sew gusset lining to gusset at top edge.

8. Sew lining and gusset darts.

9. Finish lining the gusset.

10. Adhere gussets to bag.

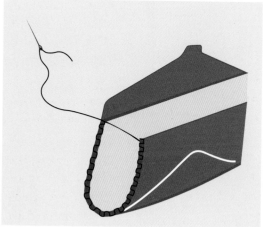

11. Hand-sew gussets in place.

13. Install the socket plate.

Dimensions: 12 inches wide by
8½ inches high by 1½ inches deep

Seam allowance: ⅜ inch,
unless otherwise noted

Fiber: Mirrabella pearlized lambskin

INTERMEDIATE

Cross-Body Sling Bag with Tablet Pocket

TOOLS AND MATERIALS

Basic Tool Kit (p. 12)

Pattern (p. 190)

4 square feet leather or 1 yard fabric

½ yard muslin

¾ yard lining

¼ yard fusible interfacing

Size 14 and 16 Microtex needles

45 inches of zipper tape, #7 plastic
coil teeth (upholstery weight), or
two 14-inch and two 9-inch zippers

Four #7 zipper sliders (if using
zipper tape)

Fabric paint (Jacquard
Dye-Na-flow in Periwinkle #812
is pictured)

Bodkin

1¾ yards of 1-inch grosgrain ribbon

Four 1¼-inch solid metal rings

Small double-cap rivets
with ³⁄₁₆-inch posts

Rivet setter and anvil

TEMPLATES

Strap, cut one,
2¾ inch by 35 inch (leather)

Strap, cut two,
2¾ inch by 11 inch (leather)

Strap anchors, cut two,
2¾ inch by 3 inch (leather)

Pouch for vertical pocket, cut one,
8½ inch by 24 inch (lining)

THIS CONVENIENT BAG with easy-access pockets is designed with a vertical pocket for housing a 7-inch tablet device. You can alter the pocket dimensions to fit another size device. The bag features two compartments: a tiered front with a zippered pocket, and the main section with two inner pockets. The front wraps around the sides and bottom, whereas the back is a flat panel. The weight of the lambskin alone is not ideal for this type of bag, so all pieces are underlined with muslin, which prevents the bag from stretching and sagging and provides the right amount of needed structure without stiffness. Custom-colored zippers are simply a bottle or two of paint away.

Prepare the bag

1. You can use either prepackaged zippers or zipper tape. If you opt for prepackaged zippers, use side-cutting pliers to remove the bottom and top stoppers, pull out the sliders, and separate the coils. If you choose zipper tape, it will be easier to insert the slider if you remove at least ½ inch on each end as well as any coil that will fall within a seam. To remove part of the coil, snip the top edge of the coil loops, taking care not to cut the edge of the zipper tape. Use tweezers to remove the remaining bits. Paint the zippers using a disposable latex glove on one hand and the paintbrush in the other. Apply the fabric paint and let dry overnight. Use an iron to set the color, being careful not to melt the plastic coil.

2. Place the muslin on the back of the upper front, lower front, and back panel. Using a ¼-inch seam allowance, stitch all around the edges to secure. On the back panel, muslin side, draw a ½-inch-wide by 6¾-inch-high vertical window for the zipper pocket. Staystitch all around the window, going through both layers. Trim away the muslin within the window. Cut the opening down the middle of the window until you get to the last ¾ inch. Cut diagonally into the corners. Place ¼-inch double-face tape on the window lips, aligning the edge of the tape with the window's cut edge. Peel the paper and turn back the edges to form the window, rolling the staystitching line slightly toward the wrong side. Place the zipper behind the window and, from the right side, stitch all around the window to secure the zipper.

Make the outer pockets

3. The back vertical pocket pouch takes up the entire back panel. The pocket edges are caught around the perimeter to prevent the pocket from flopping down or shifting within the bag. Cut the pouch as one long rectangle of 8½ inches high by 24 inches long. To form the pocket, place the short end of the rectangle over the zipper tape (the side of the bag closest to the middle), aligning the edges—pocket's right side to zipper's wrong side. Sew the seam, keeping the bag free.

4. Fold the rectangle, aligning the fold with the cut edge on the side of the bag farthest away from the zipper opening. Place the free short end toward the other cut edge on the side of the bag. Secure the pocket all around the bag edges, sewing over the previous underlining stitching lines (4a). Trim away the excess fabric from the pocket pouch (4b).

5. Make the front tiered pocket. If the zipper is in two pieces, first insert the slider. Finish the zipper closed end, binding the edge with a strip of leather. With right sides together, lay the zipper on the upper front, placing the zipper closed end ¾ inch from the side cut edge. On the zipper's open end, fold back the zipper tip at an angle so it ends at the ¾-inch mark. Sew the zipper to the upper front as far as the ¾-inch mark.

6. With the lower front pocket lining right side up and the zipper tape wrong side down, align the edges. Using a 5/16-inch seam allowance, sew the upper front to the pocket lining, starting and stopping at the side cut edges (6a). Turn the seam allowances away from the upper front, and from the right side, edgestitch the lining close to the fold, catching all the seam allowances (6b).

7. With right sides together, lay the other edge of the zipper on the lower front, placing the ends 1⅛ inches from the side cut edge. On the zipper's open end, fold back the zipper tip so it ends at the 1⅛-inch mark, folding it at the same angle as on the upper front. Baste in place (7a, 7b). With the lower front lining's right side facing the zipper tape's wrong side, align the edges and sew using a 5/16-inch seam allowance, starting and stopping at the side cut edges (7c). Turn the seam allowances away from the zipper teeth and, from the lining's right side,

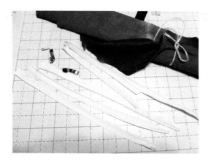

1. Pull out sliders and separate coils.

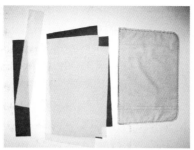

2. Place muslin on pieces.

3. Outer pocket.

4a. Secure pocket around bag edges.

4b. Trim excess fabric.

Upper facing

Pocket lining

5. Insert zipper at upper front.

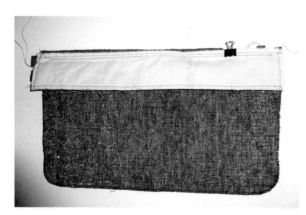

6a. Sew upper front to lower front pocket lining.

6b. Edgestitch lining close to fold.

7a. Form the tiered pocket.

7b. Baste in place.

7c. Sew in place.

7d. Edgestitch lining close to fold.

edgestitch the lining close to the fold, catching all the seam allowances and taking care not to catch the lower pocket front (7d on p. 125).

8. With right sides together, sew the bag corners on the lower front, leaving long thread tails. Open the seams. Sew the lining corners on the lower front in the same way (8a). With wrong sides facing, tie the corners together using the thread tails (8b). Matching centers and corners, use binder clips to secure the layers (8c). Bring down the lining (lower front pocket) and join the two sections, matching bottom centers, corners, and side match points (8d). Use more binder clips to secure all the layers (8e). Baste the edge, using a ⁵⁄₁₆-inch seam allowance. The finished front-tiered pocket is now ready to be joined to the pocket back section (8f).

Make the strap

9. All strap sections are cut 2¾ inches wide. Cut one section 35 inches long and two sections each 11 inches long, or measure your favorite strap length and cut accordingly. For the strap anchors, cut two sections each at 3 inches long. With right sides together, sew each strap section, using a ¼-inch seam allowance. Open the seam, and use the rubber mallet to pound it over a hard surface, taking care not to pound too close to the fold.

10. Use a bodkin to turn each strap section right side out. Center the seam. To prevent the strap from stretching, insert the same length of 1-inch grosgrain ribbon into each strap section. Insert the grosgrain (3¾ inches into each) into the strap anchors, too. To finish the ends on the strap sections, turn the edge inside, tucking in ³⁄₁₆ inch. Use small pieces of double-face tape to hold the folded edges in place. Use two strands of thread through the needle and a longer stitch length (8 stitches per inch) to topstitch close to the fold, going around all the edges on the strap sections. Topstitch the strap anchors along each fold.

11. The turn-back allowance on each strap end is 1½ inches, a generous amount to account for the metal ring thickness and allow enough room for the anvil to sit (on an even thickness) properly when setting the rivets. Use a Crop-A-Dile II to pierce the holes for the rivets at the placement marks on each strap section. (Holes are placed ¼ inch from the side edges. Pierce at ³⁄₈ inch and 1⁷⁄₈ inches from the end tip.) Add a metal ring to the strap and fold back the end 1½ inches, insert a rivet post from back to front, and add the cap. With the anvil sitting on a hard surface, position the cap side down on the anvil and place the rivet setter over the post. Use the mallet to set the rivet. Check that the rivet is secure and not in a Z formation. The twist happens when the post is too long for the thickness or the cap is not sitting properly on the anvil. For the rivet to properly nestle within the cap, the post needs to stick out of the leather less than ⅛ inch. Posts are available in different lengths; select the one that is closest to the thickness you are going through. If needed, you can always build up the layers with a piece of bag stiffener placed on the wrong side between the layers or a decorative tonal patch (see "Double-Face Leather Handheld Tote," p. 146, step 7). Continue adding the rings and rivets to form the strap. On the two end rings add the strap anchors.

Attach the strap

12. The strap attaches 1¼ inches in from the side raw edge. Attach one strap end to the left front and the other to the right back. Be sure to check that the strap is not twisted. The stabilizing grosgrain ribbon on the strap anchors is purposely made longer to distribute the bulk at the cut edges. The offset longer edges will make the strap more secure without the bulk of extra leather.

13. Sew the zipper to the bag's top edge. On each bag section at the top edge, mark the start and end stitching points ¾ inch in from the side cut edges.

8a. Sew bag and lining corners on lower front.

8b. Tie corners with thread tails.

8c. Use binder clips to secure layers.

8d. Bring down lining and join sections.

8e. Secure with more binder clips.

8f. Finished front-tiered pocket.

9. Cut straps and anchors.

10. Insert grosgrain ribbon.

12. Attach strap.

13. Sew zipper to bag top edge.

With right sides together, place one side of the zipper on the front section and the other side on the back section. On the right edges (left side of photo), turn back the zipper ends at an angle, and on the left edges—which will eventually become the zipper's closed end—extend the tail 1⅝ inches beyond the ¾-inch mark. Using a ⁵⁄₁₆-inch seam allowance, baste the zipper to the bag between the marked points, angling the end with the zipper tail slightly away from the seam allowance and toward the bag so your stitch line will run off the zipper tape. Sew the zipper to the bag, using a ⅜-inch seam allowance.

14. With right sides together, sew the front of the bag to the back, taking care not to catch the zipper tail in the seam (14a on p. 129). Turn the seam

allowances toward the front of the bag and use the mallet to pound the seam to set (14b). Around tight areas that cannot lay flat, place a shaped hard object, like a rock, behind the leather. Small pieces of hardwood are good for straighter edges (14c).

Make the lining

15. The design of the cell phone pocket was inspired by a GPS case with hard sides and soft gussets that give. The accordionlike pocket has an additional layer appliquéd at the center, which stiffens the pocket front. The fabric is cut 10¾ inches wide by 5¼ inches high and 3¾ inches wide by 5¼ inches high. The interfacing is cut without seam allowances to 3 inches wide by 4½ inches high. Finish all raw edges.

16. Fuse the interfacing to the pocket front appliqué. For bulk-free edges, first fold the corners diagonally, then fold the remaining edges, using the interfacing edge as a guide for the foldline (16a). Fold the long rectangle in half, bringing the short ends together, then sew the seam and press it open. Fold the rectangle so the vertical seam is not directly at the edge but somewhere under where the appliqué will be. Sew across the top and bottom edges, leaving an opening on one side for turning it right side out (16b). Turn right side out and press. Center the appliqué on the base and sew all around to secure it. Fold the side edges just beyond the appliqué's edges, forming an accordion-style pleat, and press to crease the pleats (16c).

17. Make a self-lined zippered pocket. Cut a 10¾-inch square and finish the raw edges. Fold the square in half and crease. The crease will become the bottom edge of the pocket. Finish the closed zipper end, binding the edge using a strip of leather to give the pocket depth. The zipper will not fully extend

across to the side edges. On one long edge, mark the zipper's starting and stopping points. On the left side, place the mark at 1⅞ inches; on the right side, place it at ⅞ inch from the side cut edges. The gap on the left between the zipper end and the edge of the pocket will allow for a small pleat, and on the right (which is the same measurement as the finished zipper width) will allow for a box corner. With right sides together, place the zipper on the pocket, aligning the edges. Place the zipper's closed end at the ⅞-inch mark on the right edge, and the zipper's open end at the 1⅞-inch mark on the left edge. Angle the zipper tape edge away from the seamline and toward the seam allowance so the stitch line will run off the zipper tape. Baste the zipper.

18. With right sides together, fold the pocket, aligning the edges and enclosing the zipper. Pin around the three sides (18a). Using a ¼-inch seam at the zipper edge and a ⅜-inch seam on the other two edges, sew around the three sides, leaving an opening on one side for turning the pocket right side out (18b). The self-lined pocket with one zipper edge attached is finished and ready to be sewn to a lining wall (18c).

19. On the wrong side of the lining, use interfacing around the pocket areas that are stress points. Add strips of interfacing across the lining (19a). Pin the accordion pleats closed. Center the pocket on the lining. On one pocket side remove the pins and repin just the undersection of the accordion. Do the same at the other side of the pocket. Sew the pocket sides, taking care not to catch the upper edge of the accordion pleat. Lay the accordion pleat flat and sew across the bottom edge, catching all layers at the corner edges (19b).

20. With right sides, together attach the zipper to the lining, turning back the zipper end at an angle and sewing with a ¼-inch seam allowance (20a on p. 131). Prepare to add depth to the zippered patch

14a. Sew front of bag to back.

14b. Pound seam to set.

14c. Use hard object on curved seams.

16a. Fold corners diagonally, then fold remaining edges.

16b. Sew across top and bottom edges.

16c. Make accordion-style pleats.

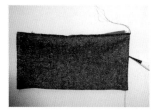

17. Place zipper on pocket, aligning the edges.

18a. Pin three sides of pocket.

18b. Sew around three sides.

18c. Finished pocket.

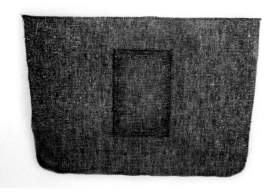

19a. Interface the lining at pocket stress points.

19b. Sew the cell phone pocket.

pocket. Flip the pocket down so it's in the final position. Mark the center on the pocket and the lining (see the folds). To add depth, baste the pocket sides as follows: On the pocket's left edge (the side with the zipper opening), first press the side into a $\frac{1}{2}$-inch accordion pleat. Then tuck the pocket side edge as close as possible to the zipper end. Match the bottom centers, then hand-baste the pocket's left side to the lining, basting only the undersection of the accordion pleat and making sure that when the pleat is folded, the bottom of the pocket is smooth across the base and the centers match. On the pocket's right edge, tuck the side edge as close as possible to the zipper's closed end and hand-baste $1\frac{1}{2}$ inches down the side (20b).

21. Starting at the left zipper end, stitch the vertical seam as far as the bottom corner, making sure to not catch the pleat/top edge of the accordion. With the needle down and the presser foot up, pivot the pocket. Lift the needle and, without moving the pocket much, gently fold the pleat under the foot and smooth it out. Catching the bottom corner of the pleat, continue sewing across the bottom to the other edge, then pivot at the bottom corner and sew up the side to the top corner.

Join the lining

22. With right sides together sew the front to the back, leaving an opening at the bottom edge for turning the bag right side out (22a). With right sides together, drop the bag into the lining and secure with clips (22b). Sew across the top edge, tucking the zipper tails into the bag so they do not get caught in the stitching (22c). Reach into the bag through the opening in the lining and push all the seam allowances toward the lining. On the lining, stitch close to the fold, going through all the seam allowances and being careful not to catch the bag or other parts of the lining (22d). To secure the lining to the bag, align the bottom corners and take a few stitches through all the seam allowances (22e). Turn the bag so the lining is right side out (22f). At the bottom of the bag, pin the opening closed, being careful not to catch the bag layer. To close the opening, stitch close to the edge (22g).

23. Insert the slider (23a), close the zipper, and check that the coil edges at the other end are even. Cut a leather piece $1\frac{1}{8}$ inches wide by $1\frac{3}{4}$ inches long. With right sides together, sew the short end to the edge of the zipper using a $\frac{3}{16}$-inch seam allowance. Wrap the leather around the zipper end until the cut edge covers the stitching line underneath. Secure the wrap with double-face tape. From the right side, topstitch all around the patch. Pierce the holes and add the double-cap rivets (23b).

24. To ensure the sliders do not pull away from the zipper, use rivets to create stoppers. Before adding the rivet, build up the layers with a patch (the zipper tape is too thin for the post to set properly). Two additional layers of leather should be enough cushioning. Create a patch from a folded leather strip, placing the fold toward the coil, so the edge looks finished. For each rivet, cut a $\frac{1}{2}$-inch by 1-inch strip. Add double-face tape, peel the paper, and fold it in half to form a $\frac{1}{2}$-inch square. Pierce a hole at $\frac{3}{16}$ inch from the fold. Trim the other three sides (keep the fold intact) so the hole is $\frac{3}{16}$ inch away from the edges. On the zipper edges, use an awl to separate the fibers to make the hole for the rivet. Insert a rivet post through a patch and the zipper tape, and add the cap. Set the rivet.

20a. Attach pocket zipper edge to lining.

20b. Hand-baste down the side.

21. Sew pocket.

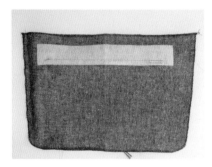  

22a. Sew front of lining to back.

22b. Drop bag in lining and secure with binder clips.

22c. Sew across top edge.

22d. Understitch lining close to the fold.

22e. Align bottom corners and take a few stitches.

22f. Turn bag so lining is right side out.

22g. Stitch close to edge.

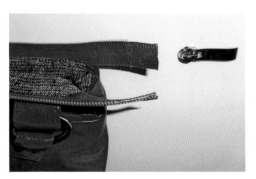  

23a. Insert slider.

23b. Double-cap rivets.

24. Use rivets to create stoppers.

ADVANCED BAGS

TOP-QUALITY HARDWARE makes for a lasting bag, and after putting in all that work, it does not pay to use inferior metals. Skins that are too small can easily be pieced discreetly to create a larger one, using woven seams in which the ends are tucked under, resembling a fishtail braid. The joints are barely visible, and when hand-sewing the weave the seam is inconspicuous and hardly visible. It is best to mark as many guide-lines as possible, using colored pens to code the lines. The old adage "Measure twice, cut once" is appropriate here because you can easily flip the pieces around, so take great care when cutting the weave lines. Painted edges add a finished touch. For more ridged materials, the solution is to precut the stitching holes and hand-sew the seams.

Dimensions: 8 inches wide by
8½ inches high by 8 inches deep

Seam allowance: ⅜ inch,
unless otherwise noted

Fiber: Upholstery leather

ADVANCED

Drawstring Bucket Bag

TOOLS AND MATERIALS

Basic Tool Kit (p. 12)
Pattern (p. 192)
6 square feet leather or
1¼ yards fabric
¾ yard lining
Scrap of interfacing
Size 16 and 18 leather needle
9-inch zipper
Eight ⅞-inch-wide screw-back
grommets
Water-based edge dye (Fiebing's Edge
Kote in Brown is shown)
Hand-sewing leather punch
Two 1-inch metal rings
Double-cap rivets
8-inch square bag stiffener
4 bag feet
2 swivel hooks
Figure-eight decorative metal rings
Two 15-inch chains

TEMPLATES

Short handle strap, cut one,
1¾ inch by 15 inch
Short handle strap facing, cut one,
¾ inch by 12 inch
Strap anchors, drawstring and slider,
cut one, 1 inch by 42¼ inch
Pouch for zipper pocket, cut one,
7½ inch by 11¼ inch
Patch pocket, cut three,
8¾ inch by 5½ inch

W ATER-BASED dyes and cements are easy to use, and allow you a little time to wipe up spills for painless cleanup. It is important to precut as many rivet holes as possible before topstitching the straps, otherwise you run the risk of cutting the thread, which leads to fraying and unraveling. For die-cut edges on heavier leathers, it is better to use a clear grid ruler with a metal cutting edge (so you can see the width you are cutting) and a utility knife instead a rotary cutter. The latter will compress the spongy edge, whereas a utility knife makes a perfect perpendicular cut. Folding substantial leathers creates a roundish edge; before folding, use a metal-edged ruler and utility knife to score it.

Make the bag

1. Use the rotary cutter to cut the bag panels. With right sides facing, sew two bag panels together. Use a mallet to pound the seam open over a hard surface. From the right side, using the presser foot as a guide, topstitch on either side of the seam (1a). Repeat with the other two panels. With right sides facing, sew the two sections together and open the seams (1b). Topstitch in the same manner (1c).

2. Mark the screw-back grommet position at the bag's top edge and on the corresponding point on the facing. Use the inside of the grommet to trace the circle. Cut the openings, plus two little triangles to accommodate the housing for the screws. On two of the panels mark the rivet placement for the short handle strap anchors, marking them on the facing as well. Use a hand-sewing leather punch to cut the rivet holes.

Make the strips and the short handle strap

3. The short handle strap anchors, drawstring, and drawstring slider are all prepared from the same strip, and the finished cut width is ³⁄₈ inch. Cut a 1-inch by 42¼-inch strip. Using a clear grid ruler with metal edge and a utility knife, on the right side of the leather score a line lengthwise down the middle of the strip, scoring through just the top layer. On the back, use a foam brush to apply leathercraft cement to the entire strip. Wait a few minutes until the cement becomes cloudy and tacky, then fold the strip in half lengthwise. Use the mallet to flatten out the strip, pounding over a hard surface to embed the glue and eliminate any air bubbles. Let the glue dry overnight. Use the clear grid ruler with metal edge and a utility knife to trim the strip to ³⁄₈ inch wide.

4. Cut the 42¼-inch strip as follows: two 5¼-inch pieces for the short handle strap anchors, one 28-inch piece for the drawstring, and one 3¾-inch piece for the drawstring slider. Use the edge beveler to skive the tip ends as follows. On the drawstring and drawstring slider, skive the underlayer for a distance of ½ inch from the tip end. On the short handle strap anchors, skive only one of the tips, shaving the underlayer for a distance of ³⁄₈ inch from the tip end. Repeat for the other anchor.

5. Use a Crop-A-Dile II to pierce holes for the rivets on the short handle strap anchors and drawstring slider. On the anchors, at the skived end, pierce the holes at ³⁄₈ inch and 1 inch; at the other end, pierce the holes at 1 inch and 1⅝ inches, all measured from their respective tip ends. For the drawstring slider, pierce a hole at the center and on each end, ½ inch from the tip end. Topstitch through the center of each strip, using two threads and a stitch length of 8 stitches/inch. The back of the drawstring will show and has only a single thread on one side, so topstitch again with that side up, going through the same stitching holes. Your strip will end up with three strands on either side.

6. Before dyeing the edges, use the edge beveler to round off any sharp corners, especially the exposed ones. Dye the cut edges, keeping the work taut (clamp longer lengths to a vise). Use the stainless-steel edge paddle to run a bead of dye along the cut edge. Apply a little at a time, working spans of about 2 inches, and use a damp cloth to wipe off any mistakes or extra drips immediately. Edge dye all the exposed cut edges.

7. Cut the handle strap 1¾ inches by 15 inches and the facing ¾ inch by 12 inches. At the short ends of the 15-inch strip, cut off a ¹⁄₁₆-inch sliver on each long edge, tapering to nothing at 1 inch above the short end. (When the tip ends are turned back over the ring, they will be narrower and will not align with the sides of the strap.) Use a foam brush

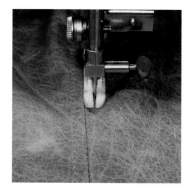

1a. Sew panels together.

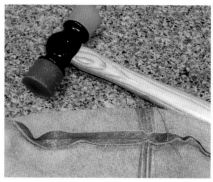

1b. Open and pound seams.

1c. Topstitch.

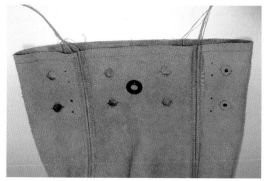

2. Mark and cut holes.

8. Apply cement around rivet holes.

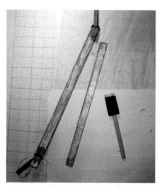

9. Insert anchor and apply cement.

to spread leathercraft cement on the strap. Wait a few minutes until the cement becomes cloudy and tacky, then fold the long sides so the cut edges meet ⅛ inch off center. Use a mallet to flatten out the strap, pounding over a hard surface to embed the glue and eliminate any air bubbles. Let the glue dry overnight. Use a Crop-A-Dile II to pierce holes ⅜ inch and 1⅞ inches from the tip ends. From the top, topstitch the strap, placing the first row at the center and another on each side of center. Use the presser foot as a spacing guide.

8. Insert the strap anchors through the metal rings. Use a toothpick to apply leather cement around the rivet holes, keeping it out of the seam allowance

(the non-skived end). Wait a few minutes until the cement becomes cloudy and tacky, then fold the strip, aligning the rivet holes. The edge will be offset by ½ inch so that when the strip is sewn to the bag's facing edge, only one layer will be caught within the seam allowance. Use a mallet to flatten out the piece, pounding over a hard surface to embed the glue and eliminate any air bubbles. Let the glue dry.

9. Insert the handle strap ends through the metal rings. Apply leathercraft cement to the back of the strap and the facing. Wait a few minutes until the cement becomes cloudy and tacky and then turn back the strap ends, aligning the rivet holes. Add the facing to the strap. Use a mallet to flatten the strap,

pounding over a hard surface to embed the glue and eliminate any air bubbles. Let the glue dry.

10. From the top of the strap, go through the existing hole and pierce the rivet hole on the facing, taking care not to cut the topstitching thread on the right side of the strap. Use the tip of an awl to push the thread to the side and out of the way. Thread a rivet post through the hole, add the cap, and set the rivet using an anvil and setter (10a, 10b).

Join the strap to the bag

11. Baste the strap anchors to the bag's facing edge. With the anchor's offset side facing the right side of the bag, place it on the bag, aligning the cut edges and rivet holes. Sew across to secure, using a ¼-inch seam allowance (11a). Pierce holes in the bottom of the bag and bag stiffener to accommodate the bag feet. Place the stiffener inside the bag. From the right side of the bag, insert the bag feet through both layers, threading the metal plate over the prongs and turning them back flush with the stiffener. To prevent the metal from cutting the lining, spread leathercraft cement on the prongs and on a leather scrap, wait until it becomes cloudy and tacky, and adhere the leather over the metal (11b). Repeat for all the bag feet.

Make the lining

12. Cut across one of the panels 1¾ inches down from the top cut edge. Stabilize the cut edges with a ½-inch strip of interfacing. Insert a zipper, using a ¼-inch seam allowance (start with 9 inches and cut off the excess). There is no need to adjust the pattern seam allowance to accommodate the zipper, as the ½ inch taken away is gained by the width of the zipper tape. Use a 7½-inch-wide by 11¼-inch-long rectangle to make the pocket pouch (12a) (see "Fold-Over Frame Bag," p. 42, for more instructions on how to insert the pocket). Add a patch pocket

to the other three panels, placing them 2⅜ inches down from the top cut edge. For each pocket, use a finished rectangle measuring 6 inches wide across the top edge (7 inches wide at the base) by 5 inches high, or make the pockets the entire width of the panel so the side edges will get caught in the seamline. For a pocket across the panel, prefinish the top and bottom edges, then baste the pocket to the panel at the side seams (12b).

13. Join the panels in the same way as the bag, leaving an opening on one side for turning the back right side out. To give the lining seams some structure, at each seam push the seam allowances toward one side, and from the top stitch close to the fold through all layers. On the seam with the opening for turning the bag right side out, stitch only as far as possible.

Join the lining to the bag

14. With right sides together, join the top edge of the lining to the bag's facing edge. Machine-sew all around the edge. Reach into the bag through the opening in the lining and push all seam allowances away from the bag facing and toward the lining. From the right side, topstitch ¼ inch away through all layers. Turn the bag right side out.

Add the hardware

15. Turn back the facing at the top edge. Reinforce each grommet with a scrap of bag stiffener placed in between the bag front and the facing. Cut an opening in the same manner as for the bag and place it between the facing layer. Position the front section of the grommet on the right side of the bag, inserting it through the holes, and add the facing plate on the back. Screw the two plates together.

16. Before attaching the strap anchor, reinforce the area behind the rivets in the same manner as with the grommets, placing a small rectangle of bag stiffener

10a., 10b. Pierce rivet hole on facing. Thread rivet and add cap.

11a. Seam across straps to secure.

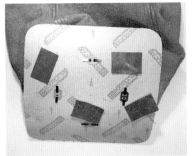

11b. Cover feet with leather scraps.

12a. Pocket pouch pieces.

12b. Finished pocket pouch.

15. Grommets.

16. Use mallet to set rivet.

17a. Anchor lining to bottom corners.

17b. Anchor lining to bottom corners (close-up).

17c. Opening in lining.

17d. Pin and hand-sew opening.

with the holes cut for the rivets between the facing and the bag. Align the rivet holes on the strap anchor with the corresponding holes on the bag. From the back, thread a rivet post through the strap anchor and the bag edges and from the bag's right side add the rivet cap. For the rivet to properly set, make sure the gap between the rivet and cap is less than ⅛ inch. If the gap is larger, build up from the inside (between the bag and facing) with additional layers, using either a scrap of leather or another layer of bag stiffener. On your pounding surface, place the rivet with the cap toward the anvil and use the mallet to set the rivet. Be careful not to hammer too hard so you don't flatten the cap.

Close up the lining

17. Turn the bag lining right side out, reach into the bottom of the bag, and anchor the lining to the

bag at the bottom corners (17a, 17b on p. 139). Pin the edge closed and hand-sew the opening in the lining (17c, 17d on p. 139).

Add the drawstring and slider

18. Use a toothpick to add a dab of leathercraft cement at the slider tip ends and just to the left of the rivet hole at the center. Wait a few minutes until the cement becomes cloudy and tacky (18a). Form a loop with the drawstring. Wrap one end of the slider over the drawstring, aligning the rivet holes, and press down on the tip end of the slider, allowing the cement to grip. Add another dab of glue just to the left of the rivet hole (18b), wait for it to become cloudy and tacky, and wrap the other end of the slider over the drawstring, aligning all rivet holes. Press down again on the center of the slider so the cement can take hold. Let the glue dry. Insert the rivet post through the hole, add the cap, and set the rivet. If the rivet holes have become clogged with glue, insert the awl to clear them.

19. Insert the drawstring through the grommets at center front (19a). Weave in and out of the grommets, exiting at center back on the outside of the bag. Before joining the ends, double-check that the drawstring is straight and not twisted. At the drawstring tip ends, spread a little leathercraft cement, wait for it to become cloudy and tacky, overlap the edges, and press to adhere. Prepare and add a patch to cover the joint. Cut a ¾-inch by 1½-inch piece of leather. On the wrong side of the short ends, which will overlap, shave ¼ inch, until the skin is half its depth. Dye the cut edges. Wrap the patch around the joint and use leathercraft cement to glue the seam. Use a Crop-A-Dile II to pierce a ⅛-inch hole for the rivet post, centering it on the patch. Insert the rivet post, add the cap, and use the anvil and setter to secure it (19b). The junction here involves several layers, so depending on the thickness of your drawstring you may have to precut the holes on each section before joining the ends. Test on scraps to see how the Crop-A-Dile II handles it. Keep in mind that because of all the layers, you will need a longer rivet post here than what you used elsewhere for the bag. The post should peek out of the layers by ⅛ inch or less.

Make the detachable shoulder strap

20. Cut the shoulder guard and a facing. To reduce bulk at the turned edges, shave the ends on the guard until they are half their depth, then round off the corners on both the guard and the facing. Brush leathercraft cement on the back of both sections. Wait until the glue becomes cloudy and tacky, then press the sections together, turning back the ends of the guard and butting them with the ends on the facing piece. Let the glue dry overnight. Pierce all the holes for the rivets. From the top, starting at the edge on one end, begin topstitching (use two threads through the needle and 8 stitches/inch), first going around the edge and working toward the center. Use the presser foot as a topstitch guide. Because the back of the shoulder guard will be visible and you have used only a single thread in the bobbin, topstitch again with that side up, going through the same stitching holes. Pull all threads to where they can be hidden, tie them, thread a needle, and bury them. Dye the edges all around.

21. Prepare the swivel-hook anchors. Brush on leathercraft cement and wait until it becomes cloudy and tacky. With right sides together, adhere the layers and let the glue dry. Dye the cut edges. On each anchor, pierce the rivet holes. Insert an anchor through the swivel-hook ring, fold it in half, sandwiching the last link on the chain, insert a rivet post, and add the cap. Use an anvil and a setter to set the rivet.

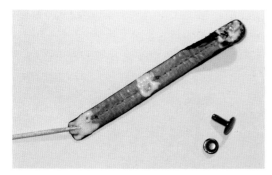

18a. Add cement.

18b. Add glue to left of rivet hole.

19a. Insert drawstring.

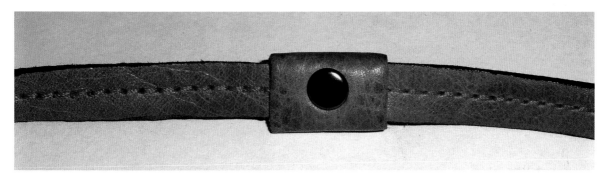

19b. Joined drawstring ends.

20. Shoulder strap guard, ready to be attached to the chain.

22a. Attach chain to figure-eight metal ring.

22b. Set rivets to secure strap.

Complete the strap

22. Open the last link on the chain, and attach it to a figure-eight decorative metal ring (22a). Insert the shoulder guard tip end through the decorative metal ring. Fold back the end and thread a rivet post through both holes, add the rivet cap, and use an anvil and the rivet setter to set the rivet. Repeat for the other side (22b).

Dimensions: 12 inches wide by
10½ inches high by 5 inches deep

Seam allowance: ³⁄₁₆ inch on sides of bag
and ³⁄₈ inch underlap on bottom edge

Fibers: Kidskin and Mirrabella metallic lambskin

ADVANCED

Double-Face Leather Handheld Tote

TOOLS AND MATERIALS

Basic Tool Kit (p. 12)

Pattern (p. 194)

7 square feet leather of each pink and metallic or 1½ yards nonraveling fabric

14 inches of zipper tape, #3 metal teeth

#3 metal zipper slider

Scraps of bag stiffener

Contact adhesive spray

Stainless-steel edge paddle

4 filigree oval charms

Paint for leather (Tandy® Eco-Flo Hi-Lite in Gold Frost #2608-20 is shown)

Small double-cap rivets

Adhesive dot roller

Metallic spray paint

Hardware for anchor at zipper end

Hardware for top of tassel

TEMPLATE

Patch pocket, cut two, 9 inch by 6⅛ inch (one pink and one metallic leather)

THIS BAG is made from two layers of tissue lambskin leather that are fused together and treated as one. Gluing the layers makes a too-thin skin robust enough for the design. All cut edges are painted with a stain. This bag features an arched upper edge with a zipper closure, flared front and back panels, V-shaped side gussets, and a patch pocket on one side. The topstitched handle straps attach to lacy oval charms with a filigree design and fasten to the support patches on the bag. The rectangular base is narrower than the bag bottom, so the gusset corners are sewn to a thinner edge instead of at an intersection seam.

Prepare the bag

1. Place the pattern on the pink leather and use a rotary cutter to cut all the pieces for one bag layer. Place the pink set of pieces on top of the gold, mirroring the pieces. Cut around each piece, leaving a ⅛-inch border. Having that little bit of extra leather around each piece will make it easier to glue the sections together, and you won't have to worry about lining up the cut edges exactly. To reduce bulk at the tassel-wrapped end, trim ¼ inch from one of the short ends on the pink layer.

   NOTE To prepare the straps, a single rectangle is fused *and then* the individual straps are cut from it.

2. In a well-ventilated area, cover your surface with clean paper and protect the surrounding area with newspaper. Arrange all the pieces, wrong side up, as close as possible without overlapping. Shake contact adhesive spray very well before using. Spray the pieces from 10 inches to 14 inches away, using a side-to-side motion. Let the pieces sit until they become tacky, then join each piece with its corresponding section, wrong sides together.

3. Lay the pattern piece on top of the fused leather (3a). To prevent the pattern and leather from shifting while cutting, place a cloth weight on top. For a razor-sharp cut, position a steel ruler with a cork back at the pattern's edge and trim with a rotary cutter. If the two layers are too thick for the rotary cutter, switch to a utility knife (3b).

Make the strap

4. Create patches to stabilize the strap attachment points so the straps do not tear out. This bag is finished inside, so there is no place to hide the interfacing; therefore, the reinforcement mechanics are placed on the surface and disguised as decorative patches. The strap support patches are made with a layer of bag stiffener sandwiched between two layers of leather. To keep the edges thin, the stiffener is cut smaller than the leather. Use the utility knife to cut the stiffener and the rotary blade to cut the leather. For each patch cut one piece of bag stiffener (1½ inches by 2¾ inches) and two pieces of leather (2 inches by 3¼ inches). Place the oval charm on the stiffener and mark the location where you will add the rivets. Use a foam brush to spread leathercraft cement on the back of one of the leather pieces. Wait a few minutes until it is cloudy and tacky, and adhere the stiffener (with the rivet hole marks facing up so you can see them). Use a Crop-A-Dile II or ⅛-inch hole puncher to cut the holes. Repeat with the other three patches.

5. With a clear grid ruler with a metal edge and a rotary cutter, trim the leather all around, leaving a ¹/₁₆-inch border between the leather and stiffener. Use leathercraft cement to glue the facing to the patch, in the same manner as described in step 4, and trim flush following the previous cut edge. Finish cutting the rivet holes, going through the ones pierced earlier (5a, 5b). Use the color stain to paint the edges all around. Dip the stainless-steel edge paddle into the paint, barely touching it, and pick up a minuscule amount (you can always pick up more). Working a small section at a time, dab the leather edge to release the paint. Once all the paint is gone from the paddle, pick up more and continue in the same manner. As you paint the edge, check both sides often for any drips. Use a damp cloth to wipe off any excess paint immediately. Let the edges dry overnight, then add another coat. The stain will fill any gaps between the edges, so if you see some voids, add a third coat until the edge is totally smooth.

6. Using a clear grid ruler with a metal edge and a utility knife, cut two 1¼-inch-wide by 21-inch-long straps. Use a Crop-A-Dile II or ⅛-inch hole puncher to pierce the holes for the metal rivets. For consistency in spacing the holes, use a template (6a). The holes are ¼ inch from the sides and ⅜ inch and 2½ inches from the bottom edge, respectively. Top-

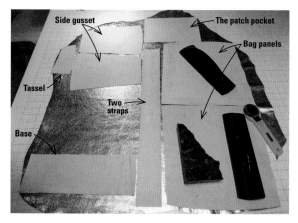

1. Cut bag pieces.

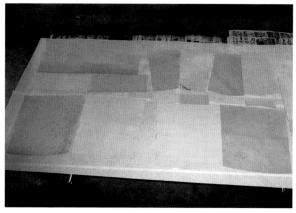

2. Spray pieces with contact adhesive spray.

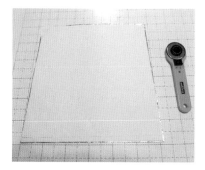

3a. Lay pattern piece on fused leather.

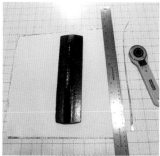

3b. Use cloth weight to prevent shifting.

5a. Patches to stabilize strap at different stages. 5b. Rivet holes.

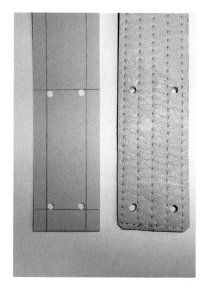

6a. Template for spacing holes.

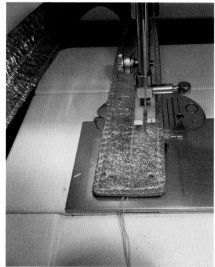

6b. Topstitch strap.

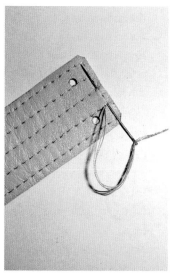

6c. Pull and trim loose tails.

stitch the strap; starting on one edge, go all the way around, stitch down the center, and add an additional row on each side of the center (6b on p. 145). Pull all the loose threads to the back, thread them on a needle, insert the needle into an existing hole between the leather layers, and exit through another hole (6c on p. 145). Trim the thread tails. Paint all around the strap edges, adding a second coat and letting it dry between coats.

7. The decorative rings attach to the strap with double-cap rivets. The strap layers are too thin to accommodate the post, so use two additional layers of bag stiffener per strap to build up the width between the straps. Cut a ½-inch by 10-inch strip of bag stiffener, draw a line every 1¼ inches, and cut the pieces apart. Place the template on top of each section, centering the holes within the ½ inch, and trace the holes. Pierce the holes and trim the ends so they are narrower than the strap. Round off the ends. On four of the pieces, grade one layer, trimming all around so it is slightly narrower. Spread the leathercraft cement around the holes on the strap and wait a few minutes for it become cloudy and tacky. On each strap adhere two sections of bag stiffener, stacking the smaller piece over the larger one. Add a dab more cement, carefully insert the decorative ring (make sure you don't get glue on it), and fold the end of the strap back, matching the rivet holes. Press the ends together so the cement can grasp. Repeat with all the decorative rings.

8. Thread the rivet stud post through the holes on the strap and add the cap. Place the cap down on the anvil, overlay the rivet setter, and use the mallet to tap the setter.

Make the bag

9. Use the stainless-steel edge paddle to apply the color stain across the bag's top edges, across the long edges on the base piece, and on all four edges of the patch pocket. Add a second coat.

10. Use a Crop-A-Dile II to pierce holes to accommodate the rivets on the patch pocket's top edge and their corresponding holes on the bag panel, and on the bag where the straps and bag feet will attach. Make the bag feet by building up the leather layers to accommodate the rivet post height. There are four squares on the outside and four on the inside, and each one is made with a layer of bag stiffener and two layers of leather. To ensure the hole for the rivet is pierced perfectly on center, start with a larger square, cut the hole, and trim evenly around the square. For the eight feet you will need to cut sixteen 1-inch squares from leather and eight 1-inch squares from bag stiffener. Brush leathercraft cement on all the pieces, wait for it to become cloudy and tacky. For every foot, sandwich one piece of stiffener between two layers of leather. Press to allow the cement to grab and let it dry. Pierce a hole as close as possible to the center, and use the clear grid ruler with the metal edge and a rotary cutter to trim to a ¾-inch square. Paint the edges all around to conceal the cut edges and mask the bag stiffener. Let dry, then add a second coat.

11. Edgestitch across the top edge of the pocket. Line up the pocket with the panel that has the corresponding holes, then attach. (The position of the 9-inch-wide by 6⅛-inch-high pocket is 3 inches down from center top edge.) Sew the pocket all around. Pull the threads to the underside, tie together, thread a needle, and run the tails through the layers, exiting at a hole in the stitching line. Attach the base to the panels. Add a line of Glue Dots to the seam allowance at the bottom of the bag. Place the base on top of the panel, overlapping it ⅜ inch, edgestitch close to the cut edge, and leave long thread tails. Repeat for the other panel.

12. For easy entry into the bag, you want the zipper to extend a couple of inches beyond the edges of the bag. The width across the bag top edge is 11 inches, so cut the zipper tape to 14 inches. Pull out the zip-

7. Build up layers with stiffener.

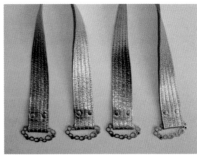

8. Attach rings to strap with rivets.

9. Apply color stain at the edges.

10. Make the bag feet from squares and pierce rivet holes.

11. Add the pocket and base.

12a. Snip zipper teeth and bind ends with a strip of leather.

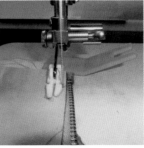

12b. Edgestitch, using a zipper foot.

12c. Sew other side of zipper.

per slider and separate the teeth. Use side-cutting pliers to snip off ¼ inch of teeth on the ends that will become the top/open edge and ½ inch of teeth on the ends that will become the bottom/closed edge. Pay attention to the orientation of the teeth (see "Security Pouch," p. 28). Use a utility lighter to carefully sear the cut edges. Cut two strips of leather ⅜ inch by 1½ inches and paint the cut edges. Add a line of Glue Dots on the back of each strip and wrap the strip around the zipper ends (12a on p. 147). Place the bag on the zipper tape, aligning the side edge of the bag with the leather strip on the edge of the zipper. Use a zipper foot to edgestitch (12b on p. 147). Sew the other side of the zipper in the same way (12c on p. 147).

13. Thread the rivet stud post through a foot, insert it through the hole on the bag bottom, and add another foot and the rivet cap. Place the foot with the cap facing the anvil, and from the top overlay the rivet setter and tap with the mallet to set (13a). Repeat with the other three sets of feet. Play around with the angle in which you lay the feet by either placing the square parallel to or at an angle to the base seam. Tie the loose threads at the base edges, thread a needle, and bury the threads within the layers, making sure the needle comes out of an existing hole (13b).

14. Reinforce each corner with an insert sandwiched between the pocket and the bag panel. To create the inserts, enclose a 1-inch-square piece of bag stiffener between two layers of leather and use leathercraft cement to adhere the layers together, as in step 10. Cut into two ½-inch by ¾-inch pieces and pierce a hole. Paint the edges all around to conceal the cut edges and mask the bag stiffener. Insert the reinforcement and secure with a rivet, going through all layers.

15. Edgestitch across the gussets top edge. Use binder clips to secure the gussets to the bag, placing the gusset's top edge 1⅛ inches down from the top edge of the bag and aligning the cut edges evenly. With the gusset side down, sew ³⁄₁₆ inch away from the cut edges (15a). When you come around the corners at the bottom of the bag, go slowly so the layers don't shift and hand-walk the stitches if you need more control (15b). Add the other gusset. If the cut edges look uneven after the seam is sewn, carefully trim so the two layers are flush and appear

to be one. When you are finished sewing, tie the threads, thread a needle, and bury the threads within the layers, making sure the needle comes out of an existing hole. Paint all remaining cut edges and let dry overnight. Apply at least one more coat of paint. Some areas may require a third coat, especially those with several layers, like the gusset edges. The paint will seal the edges and make them look as if they were one layer.

16. Line up the holes on the charm with the holes on the support patch. Insert a rivet stud post through both layers and the bag. On the back of the bag, add the rivet cap. Place the cap down on the anvil, overlay the rivet setter, and tap the setter with the mallet to set.

17. Use spray paint to paint any parts that do match the rest of the hardware (17a). Insert the zipper slider and close up the zipper. Insert one of the bead cones through the zipper end. To ensure the cone does not slide out, hand-sew a bead to the zipper tape to act as a stopper (17b). Pull the cone down over the bead to cover the zipper tape's end and stitches.

18. Make a tasseled zipper pull from a 2-inch-wide by 6½-inch-high rectangle. Draw a line ½ inch from the top edge; this will be your guideline for where to cut to. Place a slotted ruler on top and cut the fringe up to the cutting line. Sew a small ring at the top edge of the fringe; this is used for hooking the eye pin. Use round-nose pliers to open up the eye pin and partially bend it into a small hook (18a). Insert the hook into the ring, then finish closing it up. Add a line of Glue Dots across the top of the tassel and roll the edge, forming a tube. Insert the pin into the bead cone, grasping the end of the pin, and pull the rolled leather snugly into the cone. If the pin is too long to form a small hook, cut it. Use round-nose pliers to bend the end of the pin into a small loop, and just before closing up the loop insert it into the slot on the zipper slider. Close up the loop (18b).

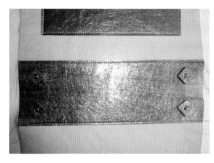

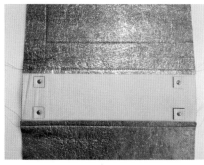

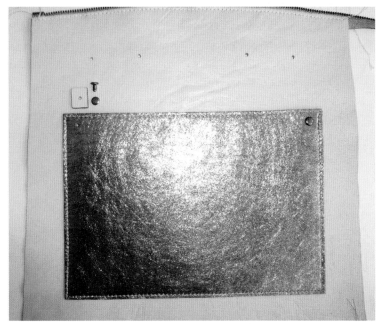

13a. Bag feet on the outside. **13b.** Bag feet on the inside. Tie and bury loose threads.

14. Insert reinforcement between bag and pocket.

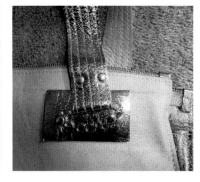

15a. Secure and sew bag gusset.

15b. Hand-walk stitches as needed.

16. Add charm to support patch and attach to bag.

17a. Paint hardware to match.

17b. Hand-sew bead stopper to zipper tape.

18a. Tasseled fringe and eye pin.

18b. Secure tasseled zipper pull to slider.

Dimensions: 12 inches wide by
10 inches high by 5½ inches deep

Seam allowance: ¼ inch on the woven edges;
⅜ inch elsewhere, unless otherwise noted

Fibers: Ostrich leg skins and rabbit fur skin

ADVANCED

Fur-Lined Mini Shopper

TOOLS AND MATERIALS

Basic Tool Kit (p. 12)

Pattern (p. 196)

4 ostrich leg skins (23 inch
by 8 inch) or ¾ yards felt

3½ square feet suede or
1¼ yards of fabric

Two 10-inch by 14-inch rabbit furs or
⅜ yard of fabric

Size 3 leather glover's needle

5-inch by 12-inch bag stiffener

4 bag feet

Clear plastic or vinyl

½-inch by 1⅞-inch magnetic closure

2 molded plastic handles

Eight #10-24 acorn nuts

Eight #8-32 by ½-inch machine screws

4½ inches of ½-inch-wide ribbon

Five ⅝-inch solid metal rings

⅜-inch solid metal ring

36-inch curb chain

6-ply DMC floss

Scraps of padded shelf liner

Two ⁵⁄₁₆-inch by 1¾-inch swivel clasps

TEMPLATES

Strap for the metal chain, cut one,
1⅛ inch by 41 inch (suede)

Anchor for removable pouch, cut
one, 1⅛ inch by 2¼ inch (suede)

Turnback allowance on the strap is
¾ inches at each end

THIS BAG, made from ostrich and lined in a plush fur with glistening frosty hardware, brings to mind a winter wonderland. Extensions make the plastic molded handles more practical; their shape echoes the curvature on the handles. The same curvature and angles carry through to the tab closure. A ¼-inch seam allowance used on the weaving edges reduces bulk and minimizes seam weight. When the weaving is complete, the tucked ends in back will measure ½ inch across. Pockets are impractical because of the nature of the lining in this bag, so the detachable bag (see the "Security Pouch," p. 26) functions as a pocket.

Prepare the pattern

1. When working with small skins, you will often have to adapt your pattern (1a). I envisioned a fairly good size funnel-shaped bucket-style bag, about 9 inches tall. I began by drawing a 5-inch by $9\frac{1}{8}$-inch oval base that measured $23\frac{1}{4}$ inches in circumference. I wanted the bag to be four panels, so I divided the circumference by four, which yielded a $5\frac{3}{16}$-inch width across each bottom panel and made the top edge $6\frac{7}{8}$ inches across. Upon measuring my skins, I discovered the pattern I had come up with was too wide. I wanted to keep the bag dimensions the same, so my only choice was to make the panels narrower and increase their number. But because all the skins had unique lines and some were wider than others, I wanted to maximize each one, and so I customized each panel to fit the width of a particular section of the skin. One skin had a prominent row of scales, and I decided this would become the center front. But I needed the scales to point down so they would not snag, which meant I had to place the top edge of the bag on the narrower section of the skin and the bottom edge on the wider section. To make the most use of this skin, this panel had to be the inversion of the other panels and narrower (1b). The particular skins you buy will dictate how you lay out the pattern.

2. After establishing the center front panel dimension, look at your remaining skins and determine the maximum panel width for the next three sections. Measure the original pattern (see the lining) and compare it with the panels you have just drawn. The additional width needed will become the two wedges that you will insert on each side of the center back panel. In the bag pictured, the center front panel is the third from the left with a promi-nent vertical row of scales, and the top edge of the bag has a chartreuse binder clip on the top right.

Cut the bag

3. Cut only the bag panels (don't cut the base yet), using a steel-edge ruler and rotary cutter to ensure your edges are perfectly straight. The edge closest to the rotary cutter is the top edge of the bag (3a). The weave cuts should be uniform in length, otherwise the weaving will be bumpy and puckered. For cutting accuracy, draw a guideline (green in 3b) $\frac{1}{2}$ inch from the cut edge. This is the *cut-up-to line*. When cutting with a rotary blade, it is hard to judge exactly where the blade will stop, so you need a second guideline for lining up the steel edge ruler, which will act as a stopper for the cutter. Draw the second guideline (blue-red in photo 3b) $\frac{11}{16}$ inch from the cut edge. I used a 28mm blade, and the $\frac{11}{16}$ inch was the extra amount needed. If you are cutting with a 45mm blade you might have to go up to $\frac{3}{4}$ inch. Draw the remaining seamlines on the top and bottom edges of each panel at $\frac{3}{8}$ inch (3c).

4. Photos 4a, 4b, and 4c show the bag as if looking up from the base (the chartreuse binder clip is at the top edge of the bag). Photos 4d, 4e, and 4f show the bag as seen from the top edge (the chartreuse binder clip is at the top edge of the bag). Notice that the joins almost disappear. The weaving has a nap, so directional cutting is important. You must orient the diagonal cuts in a V formation so you don't see the raw edges. From the top edge of the bag, the cuts will point down and angle toward the center of each panel. Draw arrows indicating the correct direction so you don't accidentally cut the wrong way (4g).

1a. Make pattern.

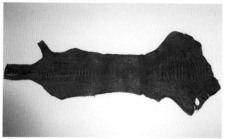

1b. Center front panel.

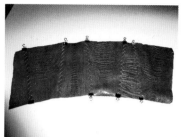

2. Determine panel widths.

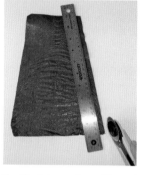

3a. Straighten edge with steel-edge ruler and rotary cutter.

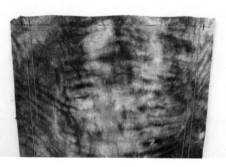

3b. Draw ³⁄₈-inch seamlines on top edge.

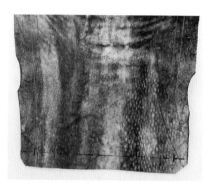

3c. ³⁄₈-inch seamlines on bottom edge.

4a. Weaving cuts are visible along the seam when seen from this direction.

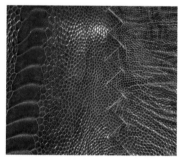

4b. A close-up of the woven seam shows the nap.

4c. The 6 panels woven together.

4d. Looking from a different angle, weaving cuts blend in.

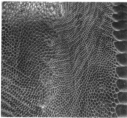

4e. A close-up of the same weave, the nap disappears.

4f. The 6 panels woven together, the weave is hardly noticeable.

4g. Directional arrows indicate the angle to cut.

5. Offset one edge by ¼ inch so the perpendicular edges align. The first diagonal cut on one panel will begin at the intersection of the seam allowance and the cut-up-to line (orange dot on the left panel), and on the adjoining panel it will begin ¼ inch below the seamline (pen pointing to the orange dashed line on the right panel in photo 5a). The panels with the offset cuts are the center front and the two wedge panels. On the wrong side of each edge to be woven, cut-up-to lines are drawn (green in photo 5b). The cuts for weaving are made at a 45-degree angle using a slotted ruler. They are spaced ½ inch apart and chevron with the corresponding edge. Many slotted rulers have ¼-inch increments; if yours does, make cuts using every other slot (5c).

6. Align the 45-degree line on the slotted ruler with the cut-up-to line (hidden from view because it is under the blue 45-degree line on the slotted ruler), placing the first cutting slot at the intersection of the dropped seamline (an orange dash). A June Tailor Quarter Cut slotted ruler works well for this step. Photo 6a shows the ruler with the slot placed for the first cut on the wedge panel. Place the steel-edge ruler on the blue-red line as a stopper for the rotary cutter (6b). Butting the blade up to the ruler will nick the ruler and invariably dull the blade. You can sand the ruler smooth and sharpen or toss the blade. Place a cloth weight on the ruler so nothing shifts (6c). Make the weave cuts. On the adjoining panel, the first cutting slot will be placed at the intersection of the seamline on the top edge and the cut-up-to line (green).

Weave and sew

7. Begin weaving from the bottom to the top edge of the bag. Insert the cut edges under in an alternating pattern. Add the next panel and weave in the same manner (7a). On the back, place painters' tape over the seam to temporarily hold the weave in place. With a strong thread, such as a button or carpet weight, hand-sew the weave, catching only the triangle points on the wrong side (7b).

8. From the right side, permanently sew the seam. Use three strands of 6-ply DMC floss to take one stitch at every corner, catching both layers. For a barely seen stitch, take the stitch parallel to the cut edge and travel with the floss on the back. If you need extra reinforcement, take a second stitch on top of the first before traveling to the next corner (8a). Use a mallet to pound the seam edges over a hard surface to flatten (8b). Sometimes a slight variation where the weaving cuts are placed will affect the crossing seamline (horizontal edge). Check the seamlines on the upper and lower edge and redraw if necessary (8c).

9. Locate the sides of the bag. Cut a strip of cardstock longer than the edge you need to measure, piecing if necessary. Using the paper, measure the circumference along the top edge of the bag, fold into quarters, and mark the points to establish the center and sides. Transfer the markings to the bag. Do the same for the bottom edge. Compare the bag's bottom edge circumference with the oval base: The more seams there are, the more room there is for discrepancy between the bag's bottom edge and the base. But keep in mind the ratio will not be 1:1 because you need ease in the bag for the base to set in smoothly after weaving. In the pattern the base circumference equals the sum of the five panels, so obviously my weaving was on the loose side, because I gained 1 inch. The base set in like a charm.

5a. Offset the cutting lines.

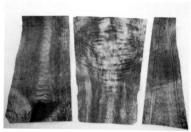

5b. Draw all the guidelines on weaving edges.

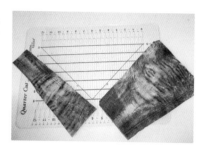

5c. Cut in ½ inch increments.

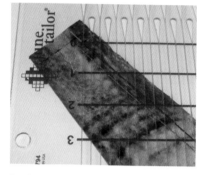

6a. First cut on wedge panel.

6b. Align steel ruler with blue-red line.

6c. Cloth weight.

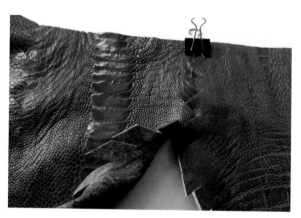

7a. Weave cut edges.

7b. Hand-sew, catching triangle points.

8a. For reinforcement, take a second stitch on top of first.

8b. Pound seams to flatten.

8c. Check seamlines. True the edge.

9. Locate sides of bag. Use paper for measuring.

Draw base to fit bag bottom

10. On a piece of cardstock larger than your base, draw lines that divide the paper into quarters. Score the lines for easy folding later. Trace one-quarter of the oval base (10a). Determine the extra length needed to fit the bag circumference. Compare measurements on paper tape measure with the base pattern. Draw a line parallel (red) to the center, equal to half the additional length needed (10b). Remember that you want your base to be smaller than the bag's circumference. Using the original base, trace the other side of the oval (10c). Fold the paper in half, and cut out the oval. (Before proceeding, be sure to compare the oval seamline with the bag's seamline; it should be about 1 inch shorter.) To mark the centers, nip the corner with the paper folded (as seen in the tan oval in the background) (10d). Add a ⅜-inch seam allowance to the pattern and cut one from the skin. Cut the base stiffener without seam allowances.

Mark the centers and the placement for the bag feet. Cut the holes for the bag feet (10e). Place the stiffener on top of the base, transfer the bag feet markings, and use a Crop-A-Dile II to pierce the base (10f, 10g). Add the base to the bag, matching the centers (10h).

11. Sew the base to the bag. Sometimes it is hard to get your hands in close, especially when working with a ridged shape. There will always be an area between the needle and the binder clips that will slip, so use a pair of tweezers to hold the edges even (11a). Use the mallet to pound the base seam over a hard surface (an anvil) to straighten it. Around tight areas that cannot lay flat, place a shaped hard object, like a rock, behind the leather. Small pieces of hardwood are good for straighter edges. (11b). With leathercraft cement, glue the stiffener to the bag base and screw in the bag feet (11c, 11d, 11e).

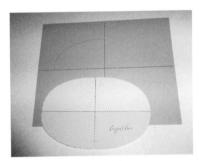

10a. Draw one-quarter of the base.

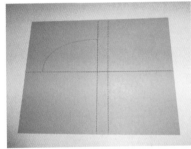

10b. Draw parallel line.

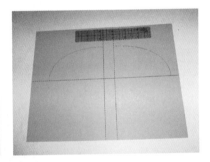

10c. Trace other side.

10d. Cut oval and notch the centers.

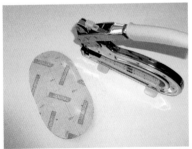

10e. Cut holes for bag feet.

10f. Cut corresponding holes on base.

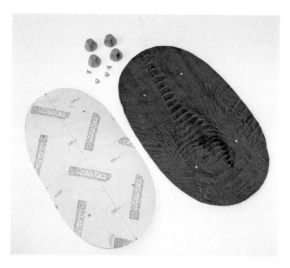

10g. Stiffener and base with cut holes.

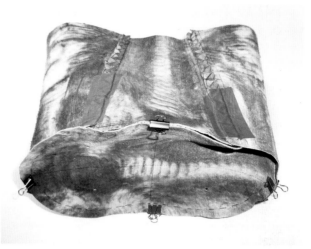

10h. Add base to bag.

11a. Use tweezers to hold edges even.

11b. Pound over anvil.

11c. Glue stiffener to bag bottom.

11d. Stiffener in bag.

11e. Screw in bag feet.

Make the details

12. The easiest way to cut the bag details is to trace the pattern section onto a piece of clear plastic or vinyl. This allows you to move the pattern around the skin until the composition looks just right (12a, 12b).

13. Brush leathercraft cement on the back of the tab closure, wait a few minutes for it to become cloudy and tacky, and adhere one section of the magnet to tab. Place the magnet ⅝ inch from the bottom edge and center it on the tab. I took my magnets from a plastic name tag holder for ease. Brush leathercraft cement on the handle extenders and wait for it to become cloudy and tacky.

14. Adhere the tab closure and extenders to a piece of suede (14a). Leave a little bit of suede all around each piece. Press to allow the cement to grab and let it dry. Cut roughly around each piece and machine-stitch close to the ostrich edge (14b). With pinking shears, cut around each piece, leaving a sliver of suede exposed (14c). On the handle extenders, mark the placement for the acorn nuts and screws (14d). Pierce the holes for the screws (14e, 14f). Screw the molded plastic handles to the extenders temporarily, so you can mark their placement on bag (14g, 14h, 14i).

15. Make the anchors for the detachable strap. Reinforce the wrong side using a piece of ribbon. Use leathercraft cement to adhere the ribbon and for

12a. Trace onto clear plastic.

12b. Place plastic on top.

13. Adhere magnet to back of tab closure.

14a. Glue tab closure and handle extenders to suede.

14b. Machine-stitch close to edge.

14c. Cut around with pinking shears for a beautiful look.

14d. Mark placement for acorn nuts and screws.

14e. Pierce holes for screws.

14f. Finished handle extenders and tab closure.

14g. Screw plastic handles to extenders.

14h. Finished handle right side.

14i. Finished handle wrong side.

extra security, use two rings per anchor (15a, 15b). Attach the anchors at the sides of the bag (15c).

16. For the fur lining, lay the pattern on the fur and use a fabric marking pen to trace around it (16a). Cut the fur lining. Use a small pair of very sharp scissors to make tiny cuts only through the base of the skin, taking care not to cut into fur strands (16b). Make the short strap anchor that will be used for attaching the removable pouch (see "Security Pouch," p. 26). Insert a ⅝-inch ring (16c). Fold the strap in half, insert a ⅜-inch ring as decoration, and hand-sew the component to the fur lining 2 inches down from the top edge (16d). Partially sew the side seams at the top edge for about 2½ inches (this will make it easier to reach into the bag and attach the handle extenders and magnetic tab closure) (16e). With right sides together, clip the fur lining to the bag's top edge, tucking in as much of the fur whiskers as possible (16f). Machine-sew all around (16g).

NOTE Rabbit fur is very electrostatic and will fly around, so have a vacuum cleaner nearby.

17. Push all the seam allowances toward the bag and, from the right side, topstitch ¼ inch away from the bag edge (17a). Use blue painters' tape to mark the top edge of the bag on the handle extenders (17b). (The handle extenders are sewn only up to ½ inch away from the top edge. I cut the 1-inch tape in half widthwise so it became ½ inch wide. One edge of the tape will correspond to the top edge of the bag and the other edge will be the sew-up-to line.) Add double-face tape to the back of the handle extenders. Temporarily screw in the plastic handles to double-check the angle of the extenders and ensure that they will lie flat (17c). Remove the paper and adhere in place (17d).

18. On the wrong side of the bag, reinforce the handle extenders' stress points by attaching a scrap of bag stiffener that is a little longer than the width of the

15a. Glue ribbon.

15b. Use two rings.

15c. Attach anchors at sides of bag.

16a. Trace pattern on fur.

16b. Cut fur lining.

16c. Insert a ring.

16d. Insert smaller ring as decoration and hand-sew anchor to lining.

16e. Partially sew side seams at the top edge.

16f. Clip fur lining to bag top edge.

16g. Machine-sew all around the top edge.

17a. Topstitch ¼ inch from bag edge.

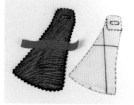

17b. Mark top edge of bag on handle extenders.

17c. Temporarily screw in extenders.

17d. Remove paper and glue handles.

18a. Secure scrap of bag stiffener using double-face tape.

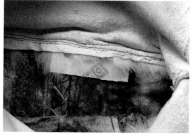

18b. Secure scrap of bag stiffener to wrong side.

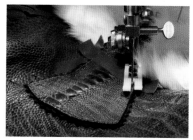

18c. Sew down side.

18d. Sew across bottom and up the other side.

18e. Tie tails and trim.

extender. Use a piece of double-face tape to secure the stiffener to the bag (18a, 18b on p. 161). Sew the handle extenders to the bag, starting ½ inch below the top edge (bottom edge of blue tape). Sew down the side, across the bottom, and up the other side, sewing over the previous stitching line you made when adding the facing (18c, 18d on p. 161). Remove the handles if they get in your way while sewing. Leave long thread tails. Thread a needle with the tails and stitch across the cut edge a few times to reinforce the corners of the strap extender. Stitching through the same holes on the wrong side, tie the tails and trim (18e on p. 161).

19. Add double-face tape to the back of the tab closure (19a). Remove the paper and attach the tab to the bag. To stabilize the tab, on the wrong side of the bag attach a scrap of bag stiffener the same way you did with the handle extenders (19b). Sew the tab in the same way you did the handle extenders, starting and stopping at ½ inch away from the top edge. On the wrong side of the bag center front, center the other part of the magnet 2⅜ inches down from the top finished edge (19c). Make sure the magnet sides face the bag. Use leathercraft cement to attach the magnet and cover it with a suede scrap in the same manner as described in step 13 (19d).

20. Finish sewing the side seams on the fur lining (20a). Attach the suede base to the fur lining, leaving an opening for turning the bag right side out (20b). Partially push the bag into the lining so the lining is facing out (20c). Reach into the bag and tie the lining and bag seams allowances together (20d). Finish pushing the bag into the lining and hand-sew the opening closed (20e). Turn the bag right side out. If you have removed the handles, screw them back on (20f).

21. See "Security Pouch" on p. 26 for instructions on making the suede insert strap. Weave the suede strap through the chain, taking care not to pull the suede too tight (21a). Allow ease so it remains pliable (21b). Turn back the ends ¾ inch and hand-sew (21c). Use two sturdy pliers to open the link, first padding the jaws with a scrap of shelf liner to protect the chain from damage. Do not use a side-to-side motion, which can weaken the link. The link is an S shape, so push the curve that is farthest away from you and pull on the curve that is closest to you (21d). Insert the swivel clasp and reverse your motions to close the link. Repeat on the other end of the chain (21e).

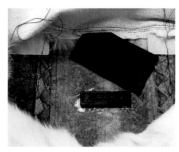

19a. Add double-face tape to back of tab closure.

19b. Attach tab closure and glue bag stiffener to stabilize tab.

19c. Center magnet on bag wrong side.

19d. Glue suede scrap over magnet.

20a. Finish side seams on fur lining.

20b. Attach suede base to fur lining.

20c. Push bag into lining so lining is facing out.

20d. Tie lining and bag seams together.

20e. Push bag into lining and sew opening closed.

20f. Screw handles back on.

21a. Weave suede strap through chain.

21b. Allow ease.

21c. Turn back ends and hand-sew.

21d. Use pliers to open link.

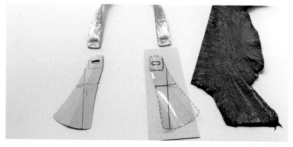

21e. Insert the swivel clasp and close link. Repeat on other end.

Dimensions: 11 inches wide by 7½ inches high
by 2 inches deep

Seam allowance: ⅜ inch, unless otherwise noted

Fibers: Stingray skin and garment-weight leather

ADVANCED

Stingray Shoulder Bag

TOOLS AND MATERIALS

Basic Tool Kit (p. 12)

Pattern (p. 198)

10-inch by 18-inch stingray skin

4 square feet leather or
1⅛ yard fabric

½ yard lining fabric

Size 16 leather needle

Size 10 Microtex needle

9-inch zipper for pocket in lining

½-inch by 1⅞-inch magnetic clasp
from plastic name tag holder

2-inch by 11-inch bag stiffener

Permanent marker in matching color

TEMPLATES

Patch pocket, cut one,
8¾ inch by 5¾ inch (includes
seam allowance)

Zipper pocket pouch, cut one,
9 inch by 12 inch (includes
⅜-inch seam allowance)

TAKE AN EYE-CATCHING exotic skin and augment it with leather, and you have a specialty bag for a fraction of the cost. This design uses only three main pattern pieces: a front, a bottom/back, and side panels that form the strap. Working with exotic skins is not difficult. Many are pliable and soft enough to feed through an ordinary sewing machine. The stingray skin is generally quite ridged, but with patience and a few inexpensive tools, the sewing is straightforward. For the topstitching, use two threads in the needle and a longer stitch length (8 stitches/inch). If the machine needle struggles to pierce the skin, hand-walk the seams. Don't backstitch, and be sure to tie off all threads.

Sew the bag and strap

1. With right sides together, sew the bag front to the back along the bottom edge seam (1a). Turn all seam allowances toward the leather side and, from the top, edgestitch close to the fold, catching all the seam allowances. Use the mallet to pound the seam flat. (1b). With right sides together, sew the bottom corners of the side panel–strap combination (1c).

Sew the strap to the bag

2. With right sides together, sew the side panel to the bag body in one continuous seam, starting and stopping at the marked seamline at the bag's top opening edge. Repeat for the other side panel (2a). Add double-face tape to the seam allowances along the bag's top opening straight edge and the seam edges on the strap (2b). Peel the paper and turn back the seam allowances. Add double-face tape to the turned-back seam allowances. Do not remove the paper just yet.

Add the closure and bottom support

3. Remove the magnetic plates from the plastic name tag holder (3a). Spread leathercraft cement on the wrong side of the flap and the wrong side of the bag front at the magnetic closure placement marks. Wait until it becomes cloudy and tacky, then adhere one part of the magnetic clasp to each part of the bag. Let the glue dry. Add double-face tape to the long edges on the bag stiffener (3b). Peel back the paper and glue the stiffener in place, aligning the long side with the bag's bottom edge seamline and the match points (see the red lines) on the short sides with the bag's cut edges. The red lines are $5/8$ inch from the short ends and align with the cut edges on the bag sides.

Make the facing

4. With right sides together, sew the facing's side seams to the strap, starting at the bottom edge and stopping at the marked seamline ($3/8$ inch from the cut edge). Open the seam allowances, and from the right side edgestitch on each side of the seamline.

Prepare the lining pouch

5. With right sides together, sew the bag front to the back along the bottom edge seam and press open. With right sides together, sew the bottom corners on the side panels, then sew the side panel to the bag in one continuous seam, starting and stopping at the cut edge. Press the seam open, and edgestitch on each side of the seam. Add a patch pocket to one side of the bag, reinforcing the stress points with scraps of interfacing placed on the wrong side (5a). Add a zipper to the other side of the bag along the top edge (5b), then add the pocket pouch.

Add the lining to the facing

6. With right sides together, machine-sew the top edge of the lining to the bottom edge of the bag's facing (6a, 6b). With wrong sides together, drop the lining into the bag, aligning the flap's raw edges and matching the facing seamline with the bag's folded edges (straight top opening edge and strap). Tack the lining to each corner in the bag. Peel the paper from the double-face tape and secure the edges in place for sewing. (The bag edges were turned under in step 2 and will not match the facing edges, which will extend $3/8$ inch beyond the bag's folded edges.)

Sew the facing to the bag

7. Machine-baste the pointed flap to the facing, close to the raw edges. Finish machine sewing the facing to the bag close to the folded edge along the straight top opening edge and each side of the

1a. Sew bag front to back.

1b. Pound seam to open.

1c. Sew bottom corners.

2a. Sew side panels to body.

2b. Add double-face tape.

3a. Plastic name tag holder.

3b. Adhere stiffener to long edges and match red line with cut edges.

4. Sew facing side seams to strap.

5a. Sew side panel to bag and add patch pocket.

5b. Add zipper pocket to top edge.

6a. and 6b. Machine-sew top edge of lining to bottom edge of the bag's facing.

strap. Trim away the excess facing on the straight edge and on each side of the strap.

Bind the flap edge

8. Cut a 1-inch by 14-inch strip of leather to bind the flap. Use scalloping shears to cut a decorative border on one long edge. Wrap the strip's wrong side over the flap's edge right side. Use binder clips to hold the binding in place. Machine-sew the strip through all layers ¼ inch away from the scalloped outer edge. On the back of the flap, trim the binding's excess leather.

Finish the strap facing edges

9. For a clean-finish look, use a permanent marker in a matching color to dye the strap facing's cut edges.

Security Pouch, p. 26

Linked-In Handbag, p. 32

Sleigh-Bottom Portfolio Clutch, p. 36

Fold-Over Frame Bag, p. 42

Trendsetter, p. 54

Trapezoid Netbook Case, p. 58

1940s Hobo Wristlet, p. 64

Clutch with Padded Bar Handle, p. 72

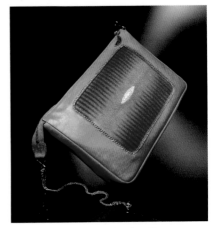
Stingray Zip-Top Wristlet Clutch, p. 78

PROJECT INDEX

Tiffany-Inspired Reversible Tote, p. 88

Studded Barrel Bag, p. 96

North–South Convertible Tote, p. 106

Leather and Suede Envelope Clutch, p. 116

Cross-Body Sling Bag with Tablet Pocket, p. 122

Drawstring Bucket Bag, p. 134

Double-Face Leather Handheld Tote, p. 142

Fur-Lined Mini Shopper, p. 150

Stingray Shoulder Bag, p. 164

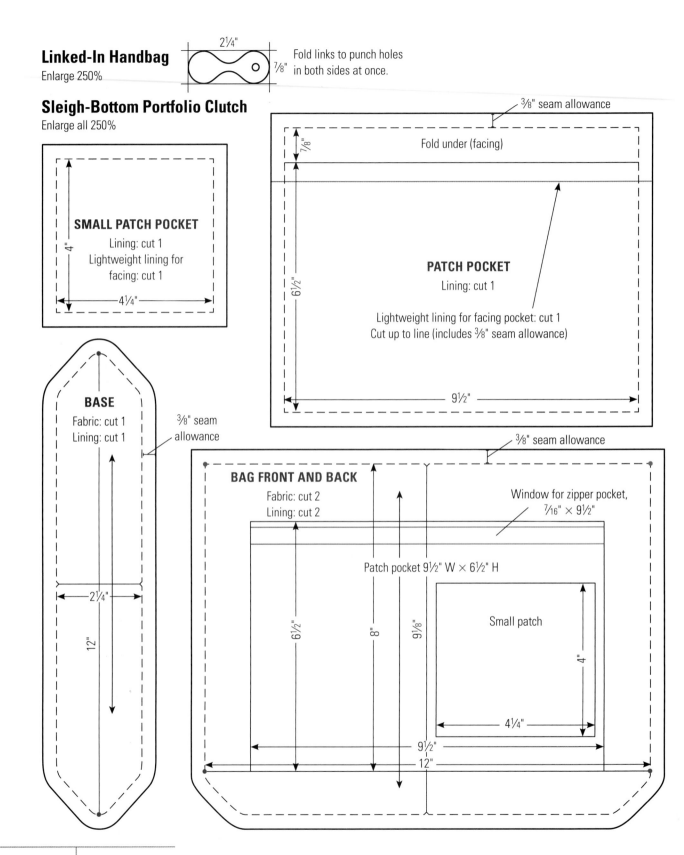

Linked-In Handbag
Enlarge 250%

2¼"
⅞"

Fold links to punch holes
in both sides at once.

Sleigh-Bottom Portfolio Clutch
Enlarge all 250%

SMALL PATCH POCKET
Lining: cut 1
Lightweight lining for
facing: cut 1

4"

4¼"

⅜" seam allowance

Fold under (facing)

⅞"

6½"

PATCH POCKET
Lining: cut 1

Lightweight lining for facing pocket: cut 1
Cut up to line (includes ⅜" seam allowance)

9½"

BASE
Fabric: cut 1
Lining: cut 1

⅜" seam
allowance

2¼"

12"

⅜" seam allowance

BAG FRONT AND BACK
Fabric: cut 2
Lining: cut 2

Window for zipper pocket,
⁷⁄₁₆" × 9½"

Patch pocket 9½" W × 6½" H

6½"

8"

9⅛"

Small patch

4"

4¼"

9½"

12"

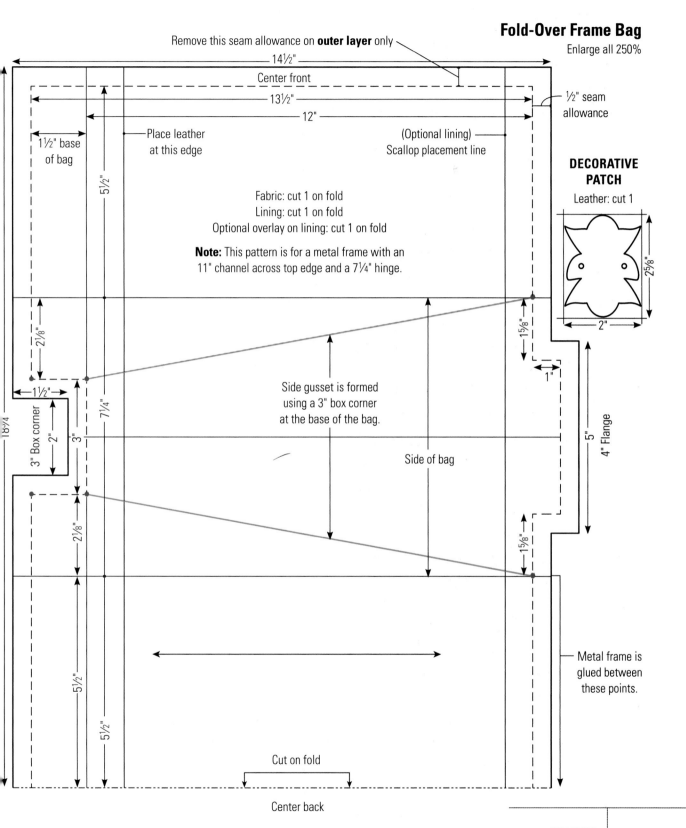

Fold-Over Frame Bag
Enlarge all 250%

Remove this seam allowance on **outer layer** only

14½"

Center front

13½"

12"

½" seam allowance

1½" base of bag

5½"

Place leather at this edge

(Optional lining) Scallop placement line

DECORATIVE PATCH
Leather: cut 1

2⅝"

2"

Fabric: cut 1 on fold
Lining: cut 1 on fold
Optional overlay on lining: cut 1 on fold

Note: This pattern is for a metal frame with an 11" channel across top edge and a 7¼" hinge.

2⅛"

7¼"

1⅝"

1"

Side gusset is formed using a 3" box corner at the base of the bag.

Side of bag

5"

4" Flange

1½"

3" Box corner

2"

3"

18¾"

2⅛"

1⅝"

Metal frame is glued between these points.

5½"

5½"

Cut on fold

Center back

Trendsetter

Enlarge all 250%

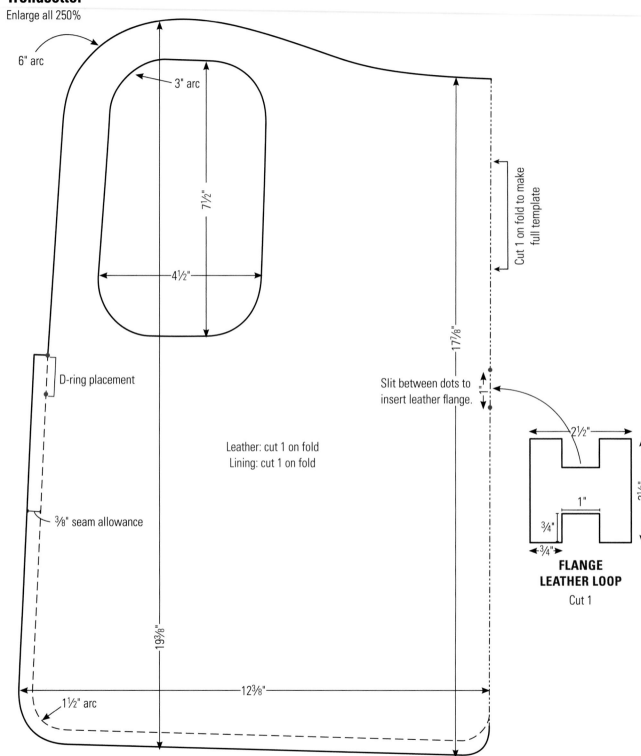

6" arc

3" arc

7½"

4½"

Cut 1 on fold to make full template

17⅞"

Slit between dots to insert leather flange.

1"

D-ring placement

Leather: cut 1 on fold
Lining: cut 1 on fold

⅜" seam allowance

19⅜"

1½" arc

12⅜"

2½"

2½"

1"

¾"

¾"

**FLANGE
LEATHER LOOP**

Cut 1

Trapezoid Netbook Case

Enlarge all 250%

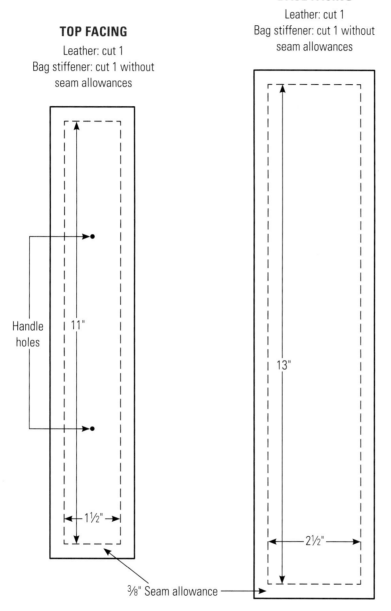

BASE FACING

Leather: cut 1
Bag stiffener: cut 1 without
seam allowances

TOP FACING

Leather: cut 1
Bag stiffener: cut 1 without
seam allowances

Handle
holes

11"

1½"

13"

2½"

⅜" Seam allowance

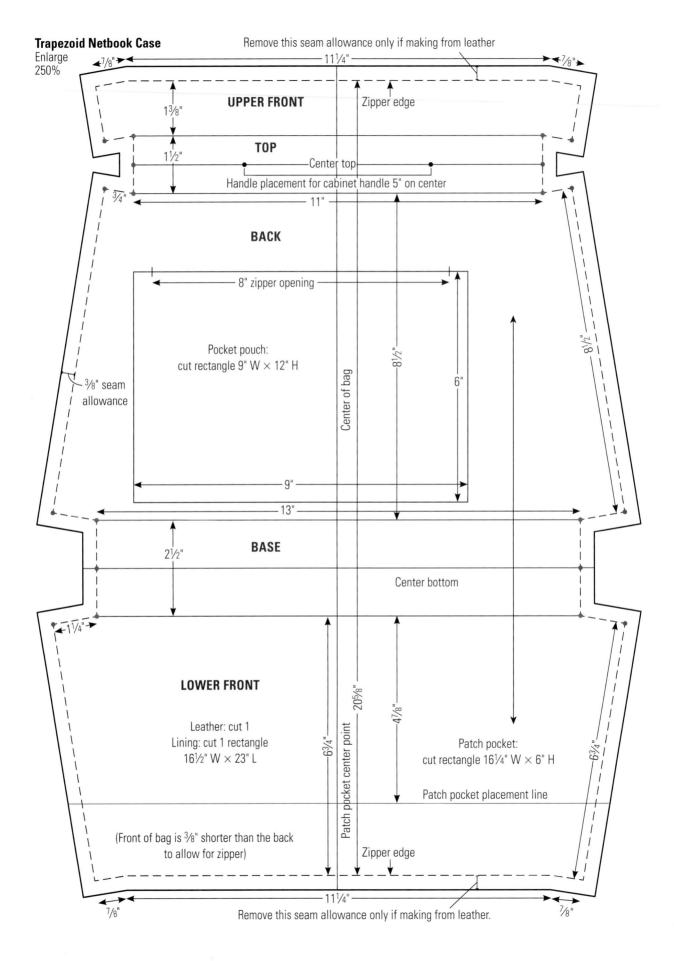

Trapezoid Netbook Case
Enlarge 250%

Remove this seam allowance only if making from leather

7/8" 11¼" 7/8"

UPPER FRONT   Zipper edge

1³/₈"

TOP

1½"   Center top

Handle placement for cabinet handle 5" on center

¾"   11"

BACK

8" zipper opening

Pocket pouch:
cut rectangle 9" W × 12" H

Center of bag

8½"   6"   8½"

³/₈" seam allowance

9"

13"

BASE

2½"   Center bottom

1¼"

LOWER FRONT

Leather: cut 1
Lining: cut 1 rectangle
16½" W × 23" L

20⁵/₈"   4⁷/₈"

Patch pocket center point

6¾"   6¾"

Patch pocket:
cut rectangle 16¼" W × 6" H

Patch pocket placement line

(Front of bag is ³/₈" shorter than the back to allow for zipper)

Zipper edge

11¼"

7/8"   7/8"

Remove this seam allowance only if making from leather.

Note: Because the two underlaps (BAG TOP edge and SIDE BAND top edge) measure differently, the SIDE BAND will stick out ¼". The extra length is needed to anchor the strap at a secondary point.

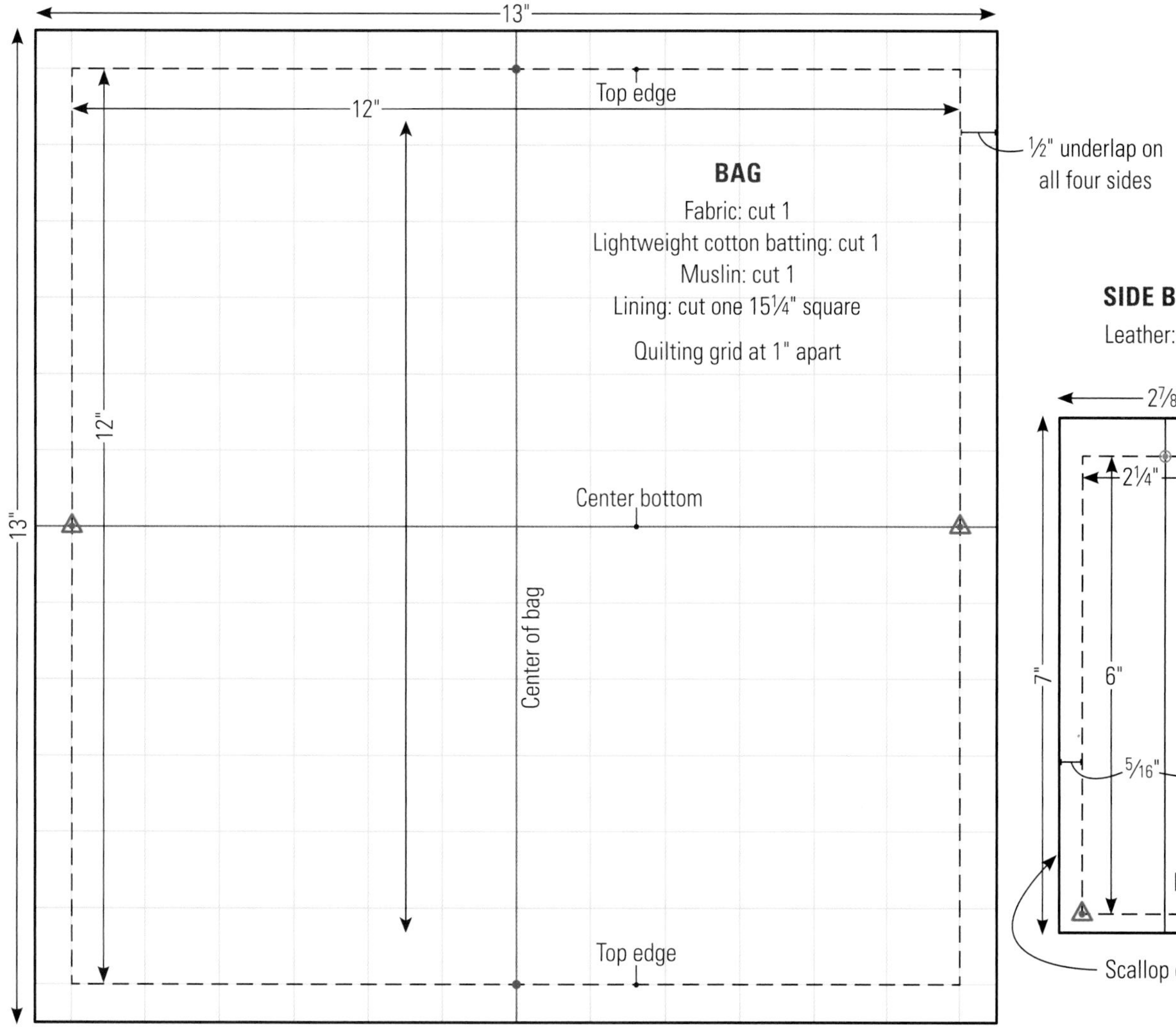

1940s Hobo Wristlet
Enlarge all 250%

13"

12"

Top edge

½" underlap on all four sides

BAG
Fabric: cut 1
Lightweight cotton batting: cut 1
Muslin: cut 1
Lining: cut one 15¼" square

Quilting grid at 1" apart

13"

12"

Center bottom

Center of bag

Top edge

SIDE BAND
Leather: cut 2

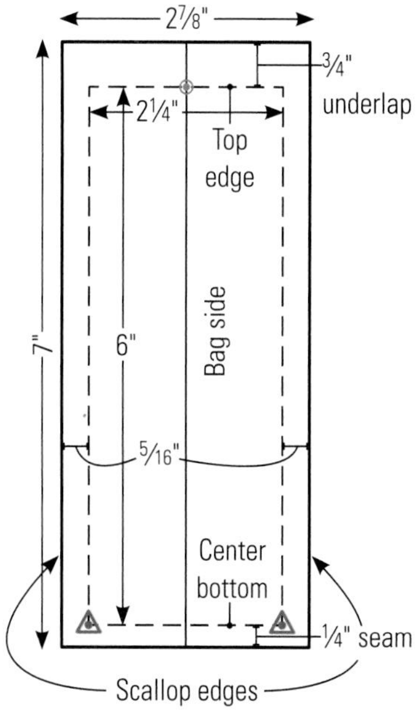

2⅞"

¾" underlap

2¼"

Top edge

7"

6"

Bag side

5/16"

Center bottom

¼" seam

Scallop edges

TOP BAND
Leather: cut 1

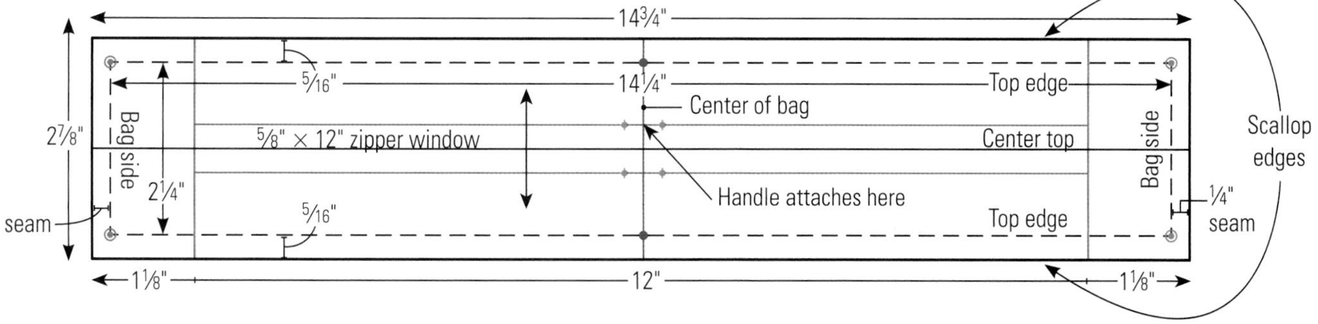

14¾"

5/16"

14¼"

Center of bag

Top edge

2⅞"

Bag side

2¼"

⅝" × 12" zipper window

Center top

Bag side

Scallop edges

seam

5/16"

Handle attaches here

Top edge

¼" seam

1⅛"

12"

1⅛"

Clutch with Padded Bar Handle

Enlarge all 250%

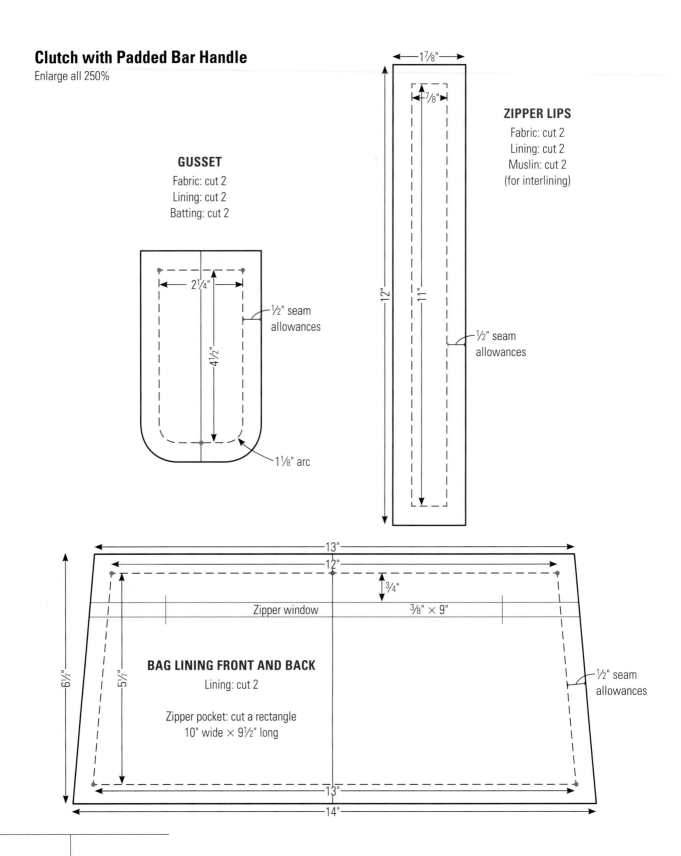

GUSSET

Fabric: cut 2
Lining: cut 2
Batting: cut 2

2¼"

4½"

½" seam allowances

1⅛" arc

1⅞"

⅞"

ZIPPER LIPS

Fabric: cut 2
Lining: cut 2
Muslin: cut 2
(for interlining)

12"

11"

½" seam allowances

13"

12"

¾"

Zipper window

⅜" × 9"

BAG LINING FRONT AND BACK

Lining: cut 2

Zipper pocket: cut a rectangle
10" wide × 9½" long

6½"

5½"

½" seam allowances

13"

14"

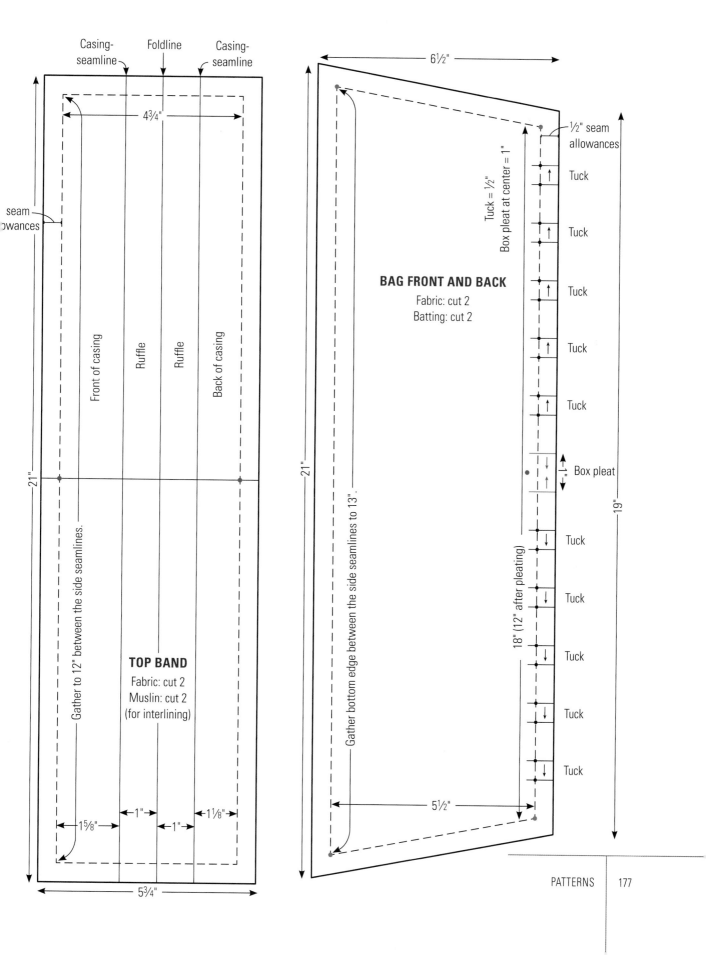

Left figure (TOP BAND):

Casing-seamline | Foldline | Casing-seamline

seam allowances

4¾"

21"

Front of casing

Ruffle

Ruffle

Back of casing

Gather to 12" between the side seamlines.

TOP BAND

Fabric: cut 2
Muslin: cut 2
(for interlining)

1⅝" | 1" | 1" | 1⅛"

5¾"

Right figure (BAG FRONT AND BACK):

6½"

½" seam allowances

Tuck = ½"
Box pleat at center = 1"

BAG FRONT AND BACK

Fabric: cut 2
Batting: cut 2

Tuck

Tuck

Tuck

Tuck

Tuck

Box pleat

1"

Tuck

Tuck

Tuck

Tuck

Tuck

21"

19"

Gather bottom edge between the side seamlines to 13".

18" (12" after pleating)

5½"

Stingray Zip-Top Wristlet Clutch

Enlarge all 250%

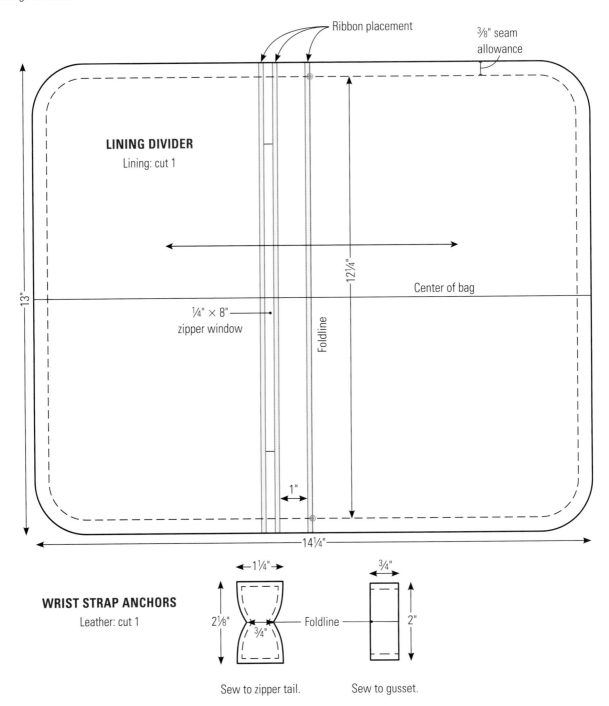

Ribbon placement

⅜" seam allowance

LINING DIVIDER
Lining: cut 1

12¼"

Center of bag

Foldline

13"

¼" × 8" zipper window

1"

14¼"

1¼"

¾"

WRIST STRAP ANCHORS
Leather: cut 1

2⅛"

¾"

Foldline

2"

Sew to zipper tail.

Sew to gusset.

BAG FRONT AND BACK

Leather: cut 2
Lining: cut 2

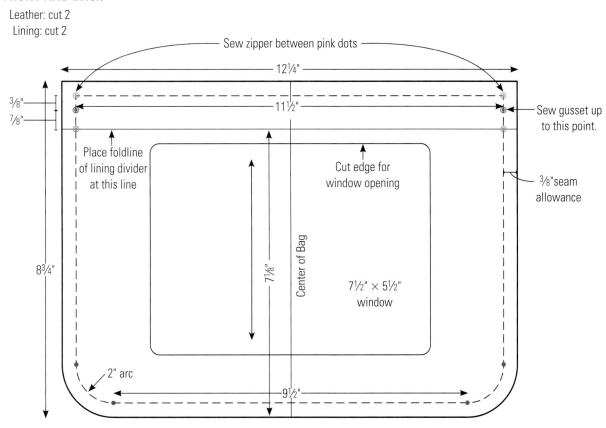

Sew zipper between pink dots

12¼"

⅜"

⅞"

11½"

Sew gusset up to this point.

⅜" seam allowance

Place foldline of lining divider at this line

Cut edge for window opening

8¾"

7⅛"

Center of Bag

7½" × 5½" window

2" arc

9½"

SIDE AND BOTTOM GUSSET

Leather: cut 1
Lining: cut 1

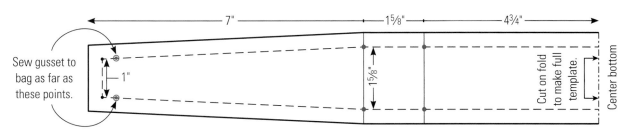

7"

1⅝"

4¾"

Sew gusset to bag as far as these points.

1"

1⅝"

Cut on fold to make full template.

Center bottom

Tiffany-Inspired Reversible Tote

Enlarge all 250%

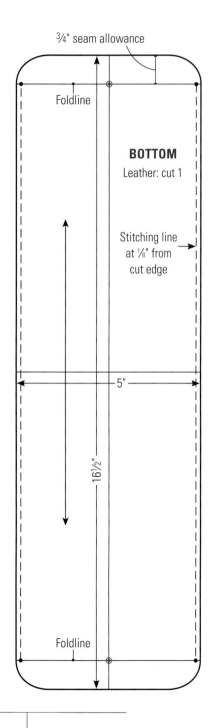

¾" seam allowance

Foldline

BOTTOM
Leather: cut 1

Stitching line
at ⅛" from
cut edge

5"

16½"

Foldline

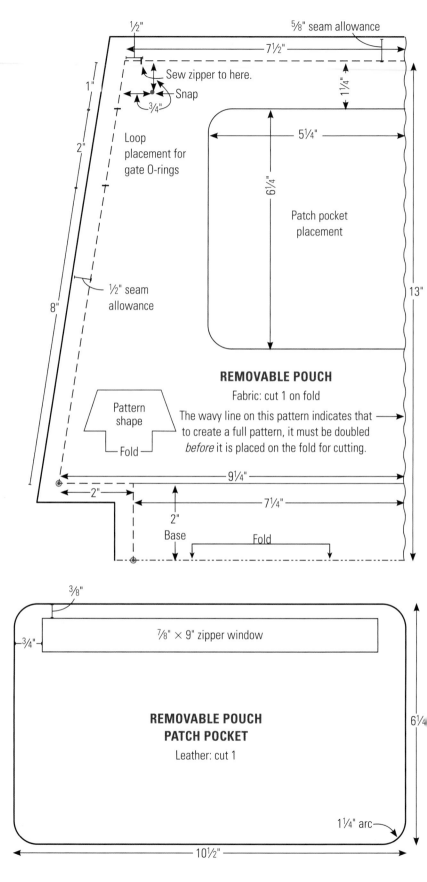

½"

⅝" seam allowance

7½"

1"

Sew zipper to here.

Snap

¾"

1¼"

2"

Loop
placement for
gate O-rings

5¼"

6¼"

Patch pocket
placement

8"

½" seam
allowance

13"

Pattern
shape

Fold

REMOVABLE POUCH
Fabric: cut 1 on fold

The wavy line on this pattern indicates that
to create a full pattern, it must be doubled
before it is placed on the fold for cutting.

9¼"

2"

7¼"

2"
Base

Fold

⅜"

¾"

⅞" × 9" zipper window

**REMOVABLE POUCH
PATCH POCKET**
Leather: cut 1

6¼"

1¼" arc

10½"

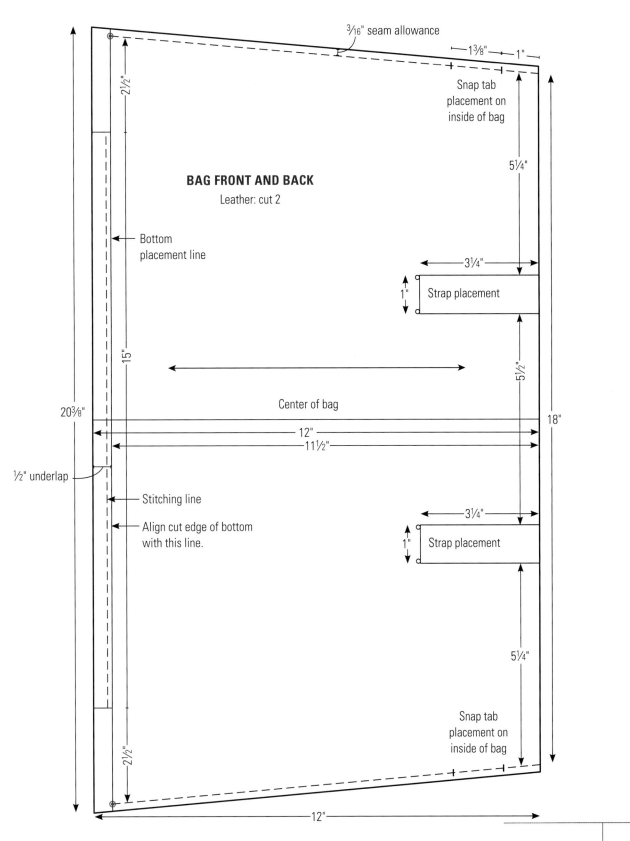

3/16" seam allowance

1 3/8" — 1"

Snap tab
placement on
inside of bag

5 1/4"

2 1/2"

BAG FRONT AND BACK
Leather: cut 2

Bottom
placement line

3 1/4"

1" Strap placement

5 1/2"

15"

Center of bag

20 3/8"

12"

11 1/2"

18"

1/2" underlap

Stitching line

Align cut edge of bottom
with this line.

3 1/4"

1" Strap placement

5 1/4"

2 1/2"

Snap tab
placement on
inside of bag

12"

Studded Barrel Bag
Enlarge all 250%

BASE
Leather (contrast): cut 1
Muslin: cut 1
Plastic insert: cut 1 without seam allowance

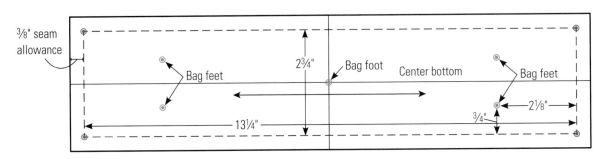

3⁄8" seam allowance

Bag feet

2³⁄₄"

Bag foot

Center bottom

Bag feet

2¹⁄₈"

3⁄4"

13¹⁄₄"

CIRCLE GUIDELINE

1½" square
1³⁄₈" circle
Snap placement

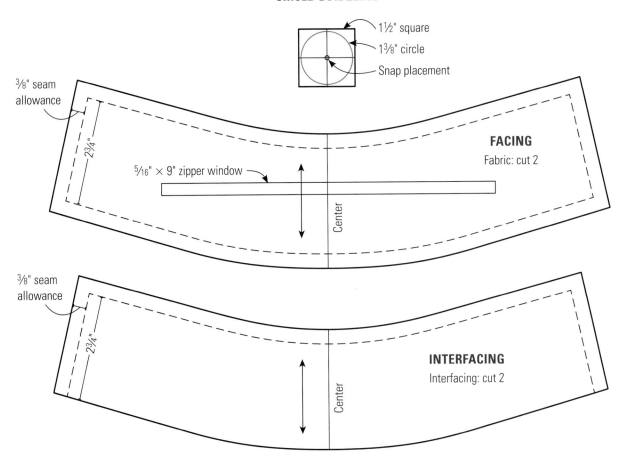

3⁄8" seam allowance

2³⁄₄"

5⁄16" × 9" zipper window

Center

FACING
Fabric: cut 2

3⁄8" seam allowance

2³⁄₄"

Center

INTERFACING
Interfacing: cut 2

LINING FRONT AND BACK

Fabric: cut 1

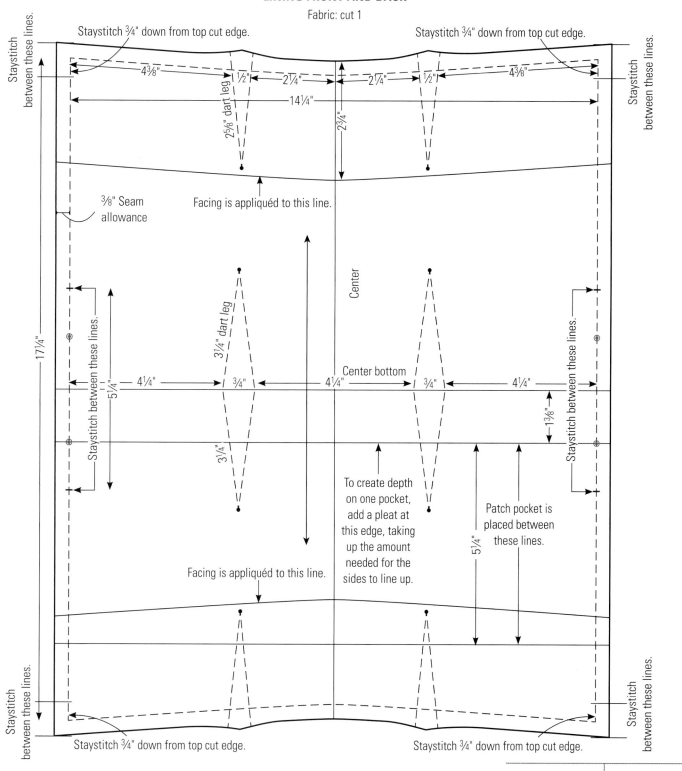

Staystitch ¾" down from top cut edge.

Staystitch ¾" down from top cut edge.

Staystitch between these lines.

Staystitch between these lines.

4⅜" ½" 2¼" 2¼" ½" 4⅜"

2⅝" dart leg

14¼"

2¾"

⅜" Seam allowance

Facing is appliquéd to this line.

17¼"

Center

Staystitch between these lines.

3¼" dart leg

5¼"

Staystitch between these lines.

4¼" ¾" Center bottom 4¼" ¾" 4¼"

1⅜"

3¼"

To create depth on one pocket, add a pleat at this edge, taking up the amount needed for the sides to line up.

Patch pocket is placed between these lines.

5¼"

Facing is appliquéd to this line.

Staystitch between these lines.

Staystitch ¾" down from top cut edge.

Staystitch ¾" down from top cut edge.

Staystitch between these lines.

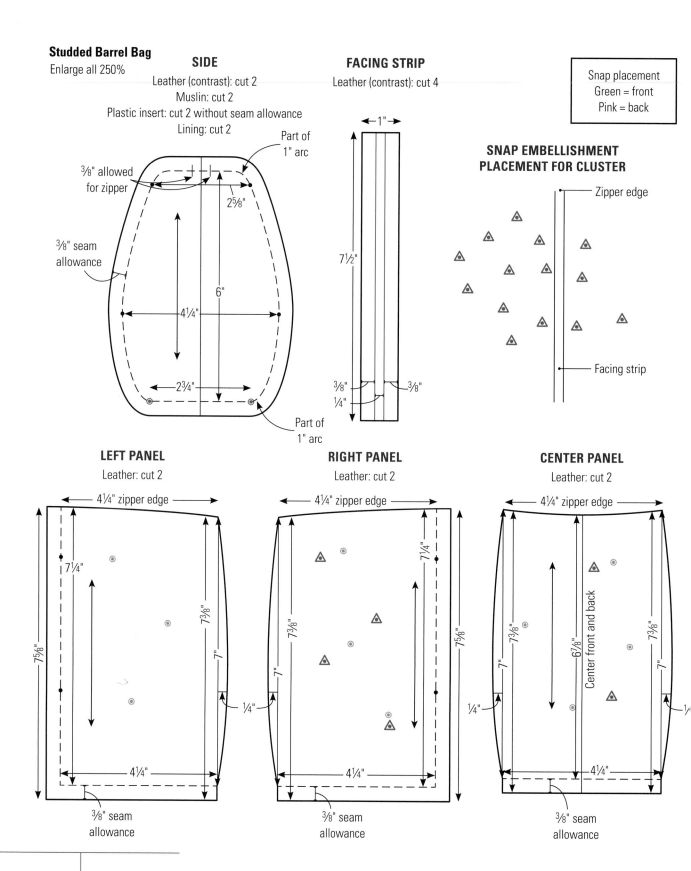

Studded Barrel Bag
Enlarge all 250%

SIDE
Leather (contrast): cut 2
Muslin: cut 2
Plastic insert: cut 2 without seam allowance
Lining: cut 2

Part of 1" arc

³⁄₈" allowed for zipper

2⁵⁄₈"

³⁄₈" seam allowance

6"

4¹⁄₄"

2³⁄₄"

Part of 1" arc

FACING STRIP
Leather (contrast): cut 4

1"

7½"

³⁄₈"   ³⁄₈"
¼"

Snap placement
Green = front
Pink = back

SNAP EMBELLISHMENT PLACEMENT FOR CLUSTER

Zipper edge

Facing strip

LEFT PANEL
Leather: cut 2

4¹⁄₄" zipper edge

7¹⁄₄"

7³⁄₈"

7"

7⁵⁄₈"

¼"

4¹⁄₄"

³⁄₈" seam allowance

RIGHT PANEL
Leather: cut 2

4¹⁄₄" zipper edge

7¹⁄₄"

7³⁄₈"

7"

7⁵⁄₈"

¼"

4¹⁄₄"

³⁄₈" seam allowance

CENTER PANEL
Leather: cut 2

4¹⁄₄" zipper edge

7³⁄₈"

7"

6⁷⁄₈"

Center front and back

7³⁄₈"

7"

¼"   ¼"

4¹⁄₄"

³⁄₈" seam allowance

North–South Convertible Tote

Enlarge all 250%

FLANGE ANCHOR

Suede: cut 2

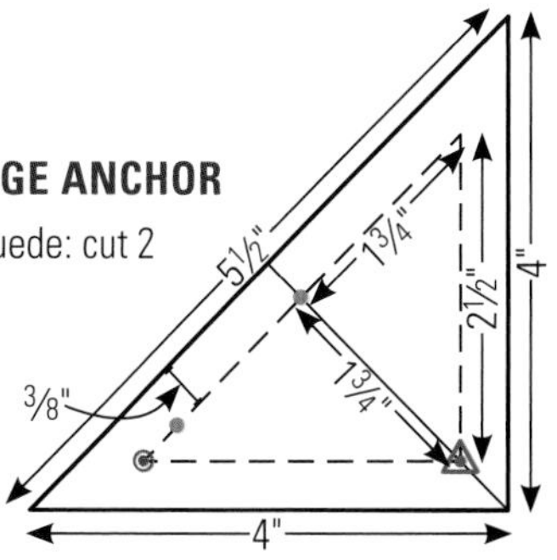

5½"
1¾"
2½"
4"
⅜"
1¾"
4"

LEAF CLUSTER AT DOWEL END

Suede (contrast): cut 4
(flip 2 for mirror image)

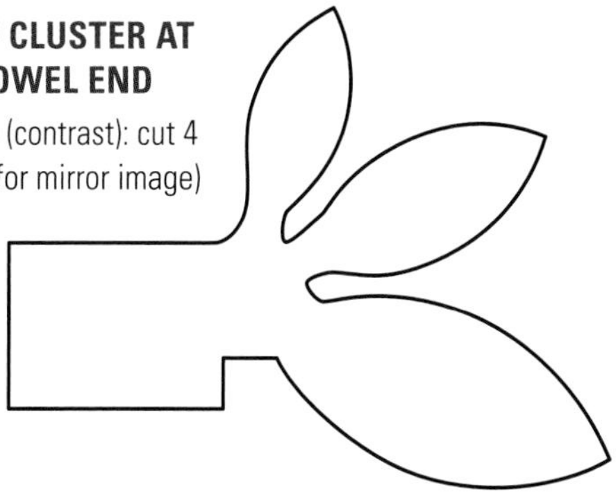

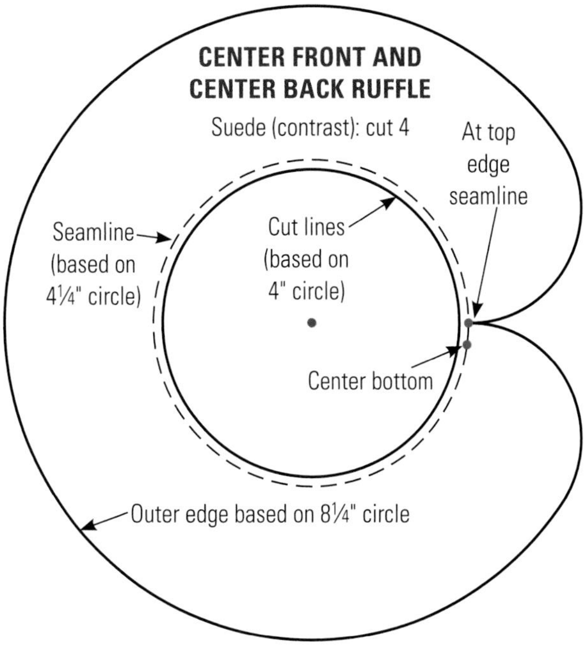

CENTER FRONT AND CENTER BACK RUFFLE

Suede (contrast): cut 4

At top edge seamline

Seamline (based on 4¼" circle)

Cut lines (based on 4" circle)

Center bottom

Outer edge based on 8¼" circle

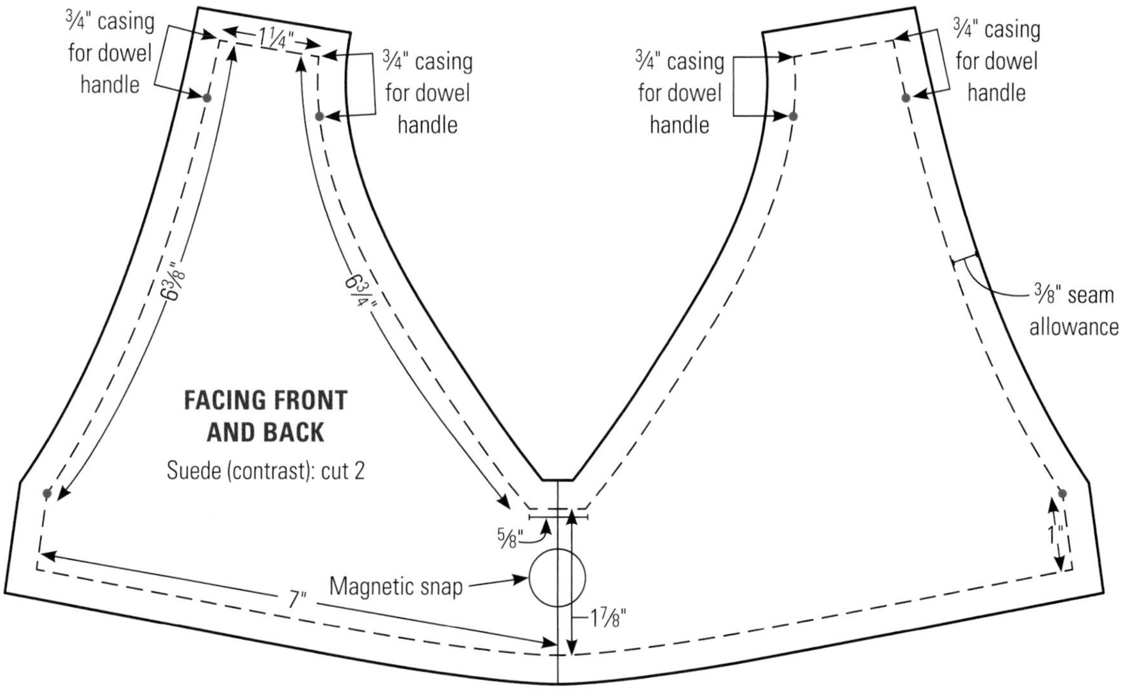

¾" casing for dowel handle

1¼"

¾" casing for dowel handle

¾" casing for dowel handle

¾" casing for dowel handle

6⅜"

6¾"

⅜" seam allowance

FACING FRONT AND BACK

Suede (contrast): cut 2

5⁄8"

Magnetic snap

7"

1⅞"

1"

North–South Convertible Tote

Enlarge all 250%

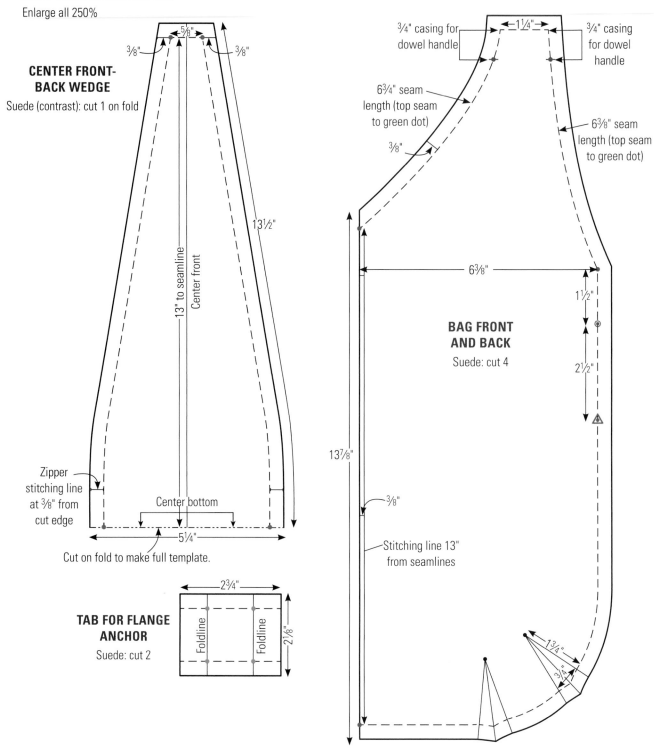

CENTER FRONT-BACK WEDGE

Suede (contrast): cut 1 on fold

5/8"

3/8"   3/8"

13" to seamline

Center front

13 1/2"

Zipper stitching line at 3/8" from cut edge

Center bottom

5 1/4"

Cut on fold to make full template.

TAB FOR FLANGE ANCHOR

Suede: cut 2

2 3/4"

2 1/8"

Foldline   Foldline

3/4" casing for dowel handle   1 1/4"   3/4" casing for dowel handle

6 3/4" seam length (top seam to green dot)

3/8"

6 3/8" seam length (top seam to green dot)

6 3/8"

1 1/2"

2 1/2"

BAG FRONT AND BACK

Suede: cut 4

13 7/8"

3/8"

Stitching line 13" from seamlines

1 3/4"

3/4"

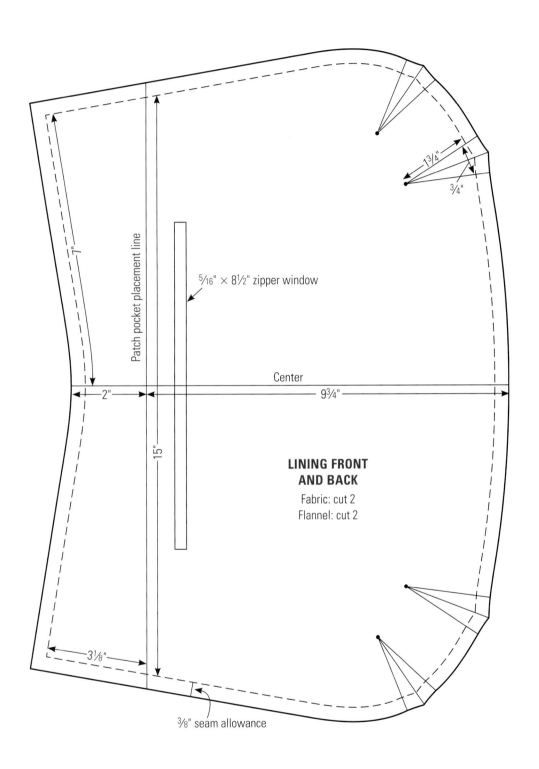

Patch pocket placement line

$5/16" \times 8\frac{1}{2}"$ zipper window

$1\frac{3}{4}"$

$\frac{3}{4}"$

$7"$

2"

Center

$9\frac{3}{4}"$

15"

**LINING FRONT
AND BACK**

Fabric: cut 2
Flannel: cut 2

$3\frac{1}{8}"$

$\frac{3}{8}"$ seam allowance

Leather and Suede Envelope Clutch

Enlarge all 250%

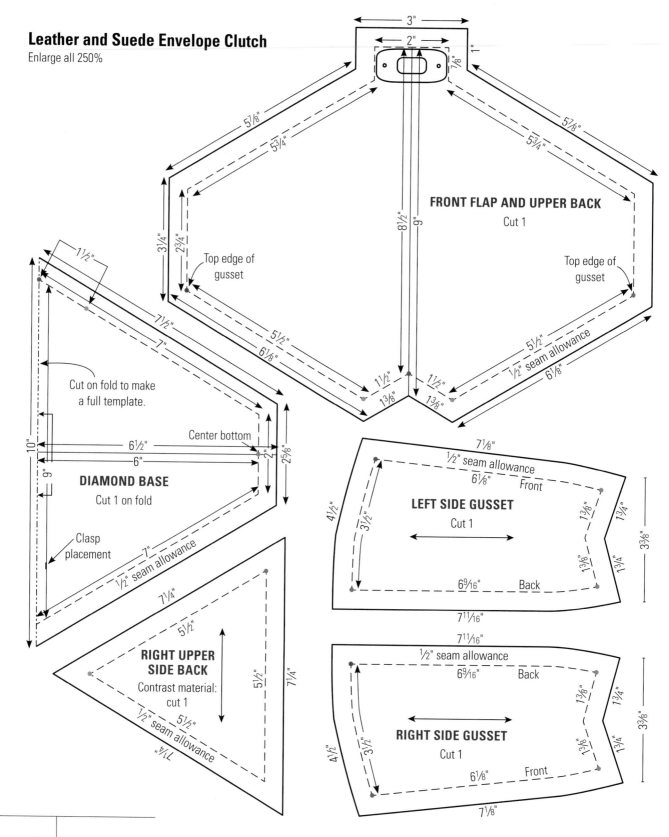

FRONT FLAP AND UPPER BACK
Cut 1

3"

2"

1"

7/8"

5 7/8"

5 3/4"

5 7/8"

5 3/4"

3 1/4"

2 3/4"

Top edge of gusset

Top edge of gusset

8 1/2"

9"

7 1/2"

7"

5 1/2"

6 1/8"

5 1/2"

6 1/8"

1/2" seam allowance

1 1/2"

1 3/8"

1 1/2"

1 3/8"

1 1/2"

DIAMOND BASE
Cut 1 on fold

Cut on fold to make a full template.

Center bottom

6 1/2"

6"

2"

2 5/8"

10"

9"

Clasp placement

7"

1/2" seam allowance

7 1/4"

5 1/2"

RIGHT UPPER SIDE BACK
Contrast material: cut 1

5 1/2"

7 1/4"

5 1/2"

1/2" seam allowance

7 1/4"

7 1/8"

1/2" seam allowance

6 1/8"   Front

LEFT SIDE GUSSET
Cut 1

4 1/2"

3 1/2"

1 3/8"

1 3/4"

1 3/8"

1 3/4"

3 3/8"

6 9/16"   Back

7 11/16"

7 11/16"

1/2" seam allowance

6 9/16"   Back

3 1/2"

1 3/8"

1 3/4"

1 3/8"

1 3/4"

3 3/8"

RIGHT SIDE GUSSET
Cut 1

4 1/2"

6 1/8"   Front

7 1/8"

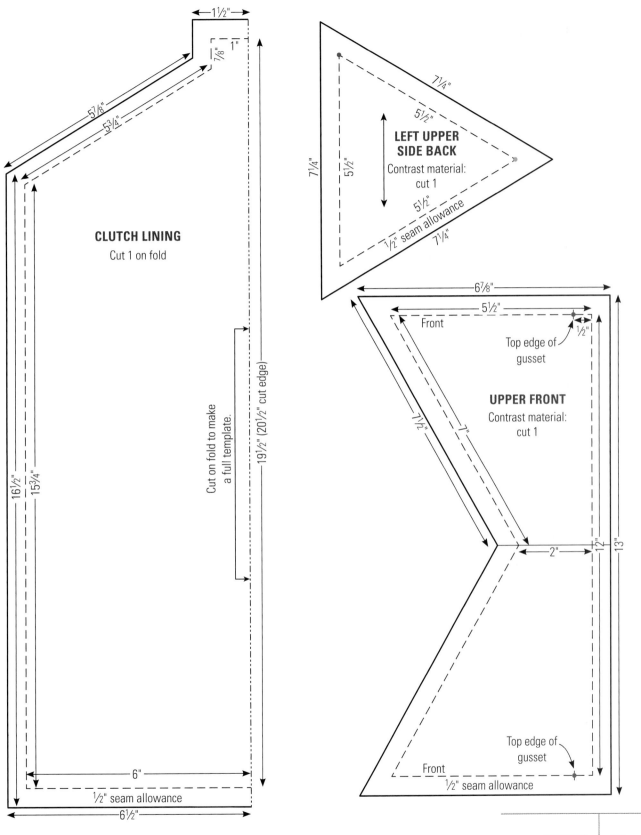

CLUTCH LINING
Cut 1 on fold

1½"

1"
⅞"

5⅞"
5¾"

Cut on fold to make a full template.

19½" (20½" cut edge)

16½"
15¾"

6"

½" seam allowance

6½"

LEFT UPPER SIDE BACK
Contrast material:
cut 1

7¼"
5½"
5½"
7¼"
5½"
7¼"
½" seam allowance

UPPER FRONT
Contrast material:
cut 1

6⅞"
5½"
Front
½"
Top edge of gusset

7½"
7"
2"
12"
13"

Front
Top edge of gusset
½" seam allowance

Cross-Body Sling Bag with Tablet Pocket

Enlarge all 250%

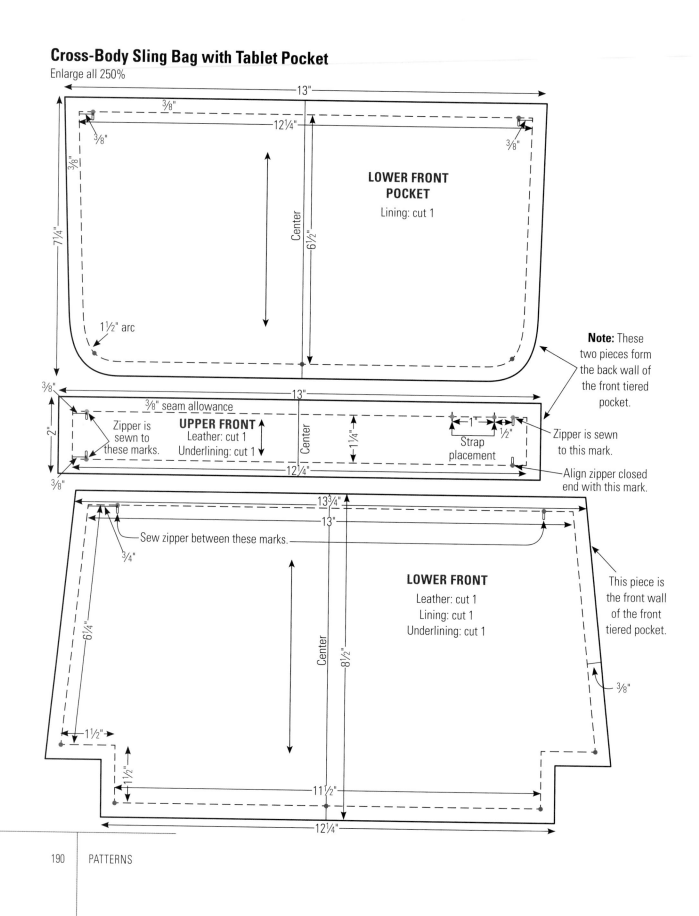

13"

3/8"

12¼"

3/8"

3/8"

3/8"

7¼"

3/8"

LOWER FRONT POCKET

Lining: cut 1

Center

6½"

1½" arc

Note: These two pieces form the back wall of the front tiered pocket.

3/8"

13"

3/8" seam allowance

2"

UPPER FRONT

Leather: cut 1

Underlining: cut 1

Zipper is sewn to these marks.

Center

1¼"

1"

½"

Strap placement

Zipper is sewn to this mark.

3/8"

12¼"

Align zipper closed end with this mark.

13¾"

13"

Sew zipper between these marks.

3/4"

6¼"

LOWER FRONT

Leather: cut 1

Lining: cut 1

Underlining: cut 1

This piece is the front wall of the front tiered pocket.

Center

8½"

3/8"

1½"

1½"

11½"

12¼"

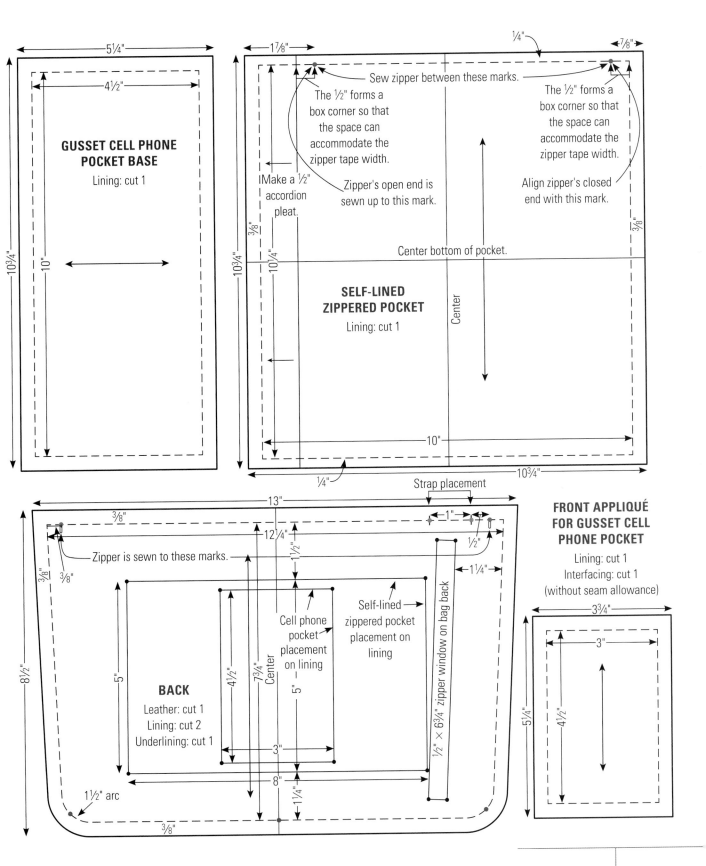

GUSSET CELL PHONE POCKET BASE

Lining: cut 1

5¼"
4½"
10¾"
10"

SELF-LINED ZIPPERED POCKET

Lining: cut 1

1⅞"
¼"
⅞"
Sew zipper between these marks.

The ½" forms a box corner so that the space can accommodate the zipper tape width.

IMake a ½" accordion pleat.

Zipper's open end is sewn up to this mark.

The ½" forms a box corner so that the space can accommodate the zipper tape width.

Align zipper's closed end with this mark.

Center bottom of pocket.

Center

⅜"
10¾"
10¼"
⅜"
10"
¼"
10¾"

Strap placement

BACK

Leather: cut 1
Lining: cut 2
Underlining: cut 1

13"
⅜"
12¼"
1½"
1"
½"
1¼"
Zipper is sewn to these marks.
⅜"
⅜"
8½"
5"
4½"
7¾"
5"
Center
3"
8"
1¼"
1½" arc
⅜"

Cell phone pocket placement on lining

Self-lined zippered pocket placement on lining

½" × 6¾" zipper window on bag back

FRONT APPLIQUÉ FOR GUSSET CELL PHONE POCKET

Lining: cut 1
Interfacing: cut 1
(without seam allowance)

3¾"
3"
5¼"
4½"

Drawstring Bucket Bag

Enlarge all 250%

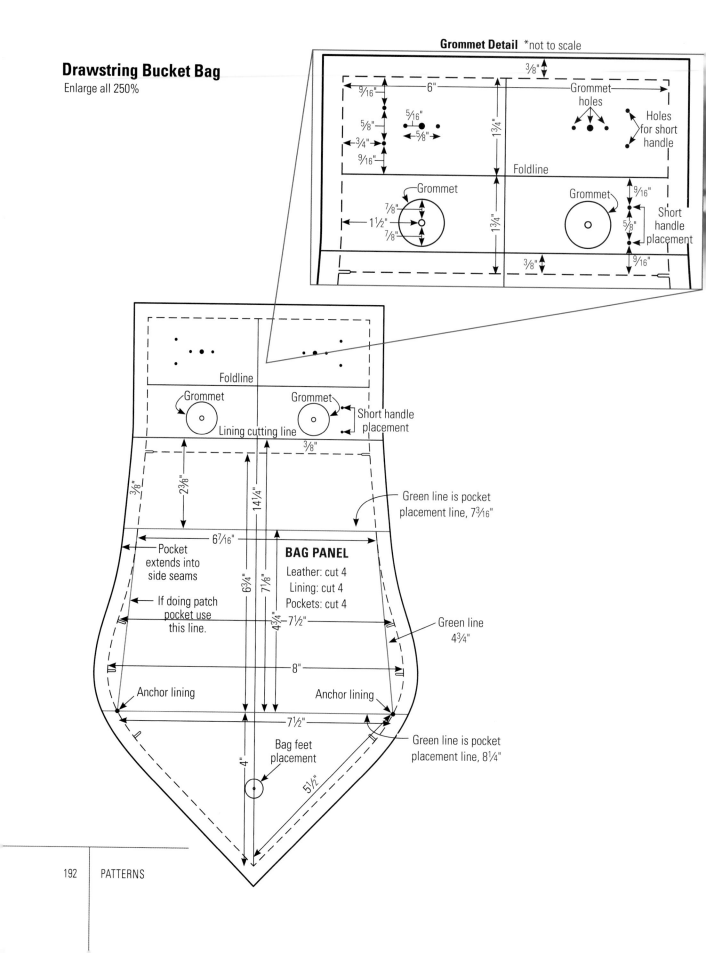

Grommet Detail *not to scale

3/8"

9/16" — 6" — Grommet holes

5/8"

5/16"

5/8"

3/4"

9/16"

1 3/4"

Holes for short handle

Foldline

1 3/4"

Grommet

7/8"

1 1/2"

7/8"

Grommet

9/16"

5/8"

Short handle placement

9/16"

3/8"

9/16"

Foldline

Grommet

Grommet

Short handle placement

Lining cutting line

3/8"

3/8"

2 3/8"

14 1/4"

Green line is pocket placement line, 7 3/16"

6 7/16"

BAG PANEL

Leather: cut 4

Lining: cut 4

Pockets: cut 4

Pocket extends into side seams

If doing patch pocket use this line.

6 3/4"

7 1/8"

4 3/4" — 7 1/2"

Green line 4 3/4"

8"

Anchor lining

Anchor lining

7 1/2"

Green line is pocket placement line, 8 1/4"

4"

Bag feet placement

5 1/2"

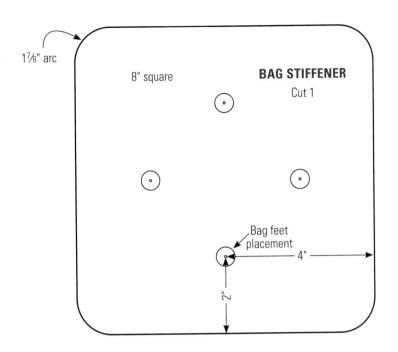

1⅞" arc

8" square

BAG STIFFENER
Cut 1

Bag feet
placement

4"

2"

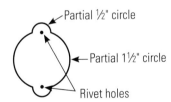

**ANCHOR CHAIN FOR
THE SWIVEL HOOK**

Leather: cut 4

Partial ½" circle

Partial 1½" circle

Rivet holes

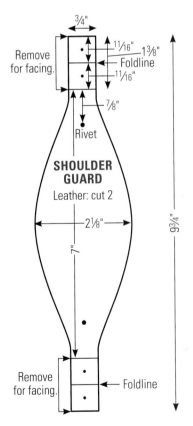

¾"

Remove
for facing.

11/16"

1⅜"

Foldline

11/16"

⅞"

Rivet

**SHOULDER
GUARD**

Leather: cut 2

2⅛"

7"

9¾"

Remove
for facing.

Foldline

Double-Face Leather Handheld Tote*

Enlarge all 250%
*Before cutting, see page 144, prepare the bag, step 1

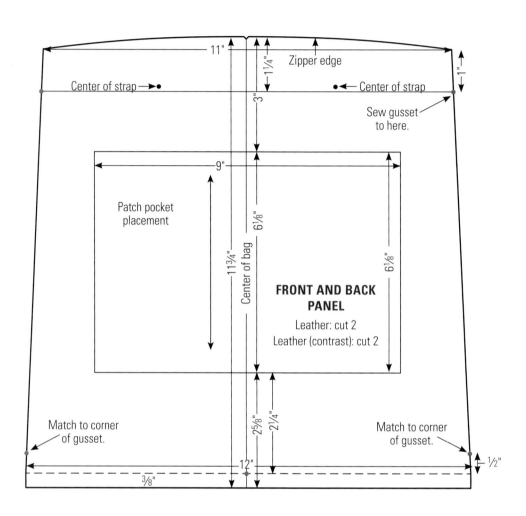

11"

Zipper edge

1¼"

1"

Center of strap →•

•← Center of strap

3"

Sew gusset
to here.

9"

Patch pocket
placement

6⅛"

11¾"

Center of bag

6⅛"

**FRONT AND BACK
PANEL**

Leather: cut 2
Leather (contrast): cut 2

Match to corner
of gusset.

Match to corner
of gusset.

2⅝"

2¼"

½"

12"

⅜"

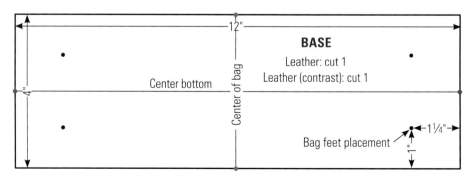

12"

BASE

Leather: cut 1
Leather (contrast): cut 1

4"

Center bottom

Center of bag

1¼"

1"

Bag feet placement

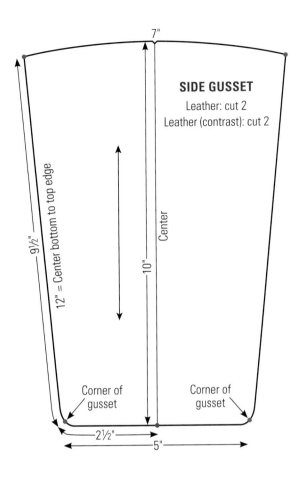

SIDE GUSSET
Leather: cut 2
Leather (contrast): cut 2

7"

9½"

12" = Center bottom to top edge

10"

Center

Corner of gusset

Corner of gusset

2½"

5"

PATCH POCKET
Leather: cut 1
Leather (contrast): cut 1

9"

6⅛"

TASSEL FOR ZIPPER PULL
Leather: cut 1
Leather (contrast): cut 1

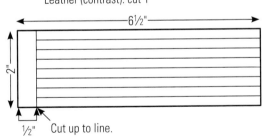

6½"

2"

½" Cut up to line.

Leather: cut 1, 3" wide × 22" long
Leather (contrast): cut 1, 3" wide × 22" long

Note: Fuse the 3" wide × 22" long leather strap to the leather contrast strap, then proceed to cut the two straps from this fused piece.

STRAP

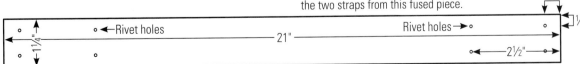

Rivet holes

Rivet holes

21"

1¼"

3/8"

1¼"

2½"

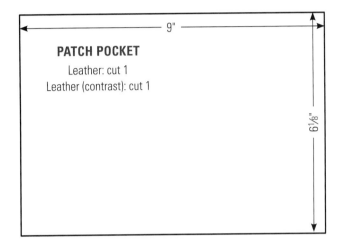

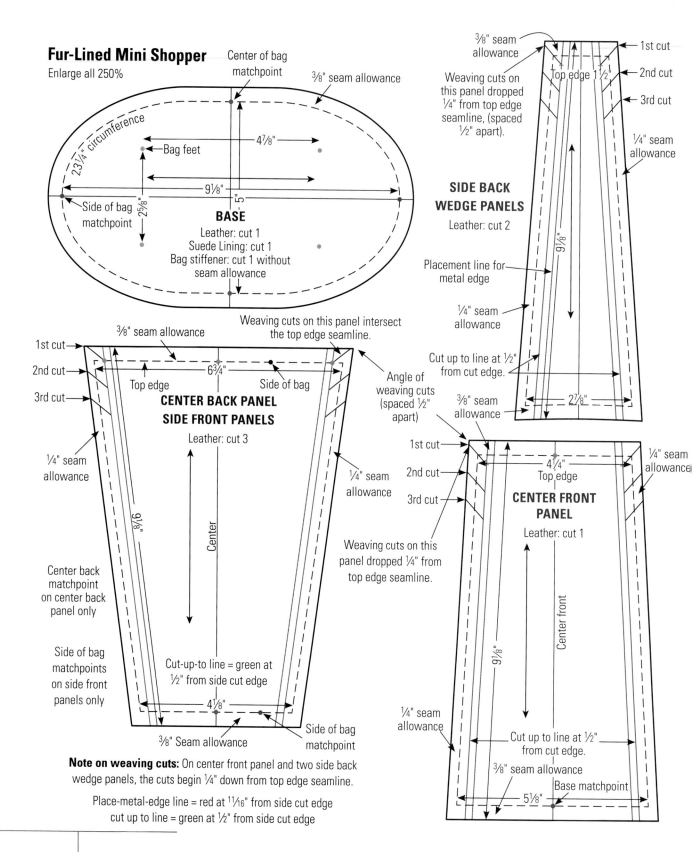

Fur-Lined Mini Shopper

Enlarge all 250%

Center of bag matchpoint

$3/8$" seam allowance

$23\frac{1}{4}$" circumference

Bag feet

Side of bag matchpoint

$4\frac{7}{8}$"

$9\frac{1}{8}$"

$2\frac{5}{8}$"

5"

BASE

Leather: cut 1
Suede Lining: cut 1
Bag stiffener: cut 1 without seam allowance

$3/8$" seam allowance

Weaving cuts on this panel dropped $1/4$" from top edge seamline, (spaced $1/2$" apart).

Top edge $1\frac{1}{2}$"

1st cut
2nd cut
3rd cut

$1/4$" seam allowance

SIDE BACK WEDGE PANELS

Leather: cut 2

Placement line for metal edge

$9\frac{1}{8}$"

$1/4$" seam allowance

Cut up to line at $1/2$" from cut edge.

$2\frac{7}{8}$"

$3/8$" seam allowance

$3/8$" seam allowance

Weaving cuts on this panel intersect the top edge seamline.

1st cut
2nd cut
3rd cut

Top edge

$6\frac{3}{4}$"

Side of bag

$1/4$" seam allowance

CENTER BACK PANEL SIDE FRONT PANELS

Leather: cut 3

Center

$9\frac{1}{8}$"

Angle of weaving cuts (spaced $1/2$" apart)

$3/8$" seam allowance

1st cut
2nd cut
3rd cut

Weaving cuts on this panel dropped $1/4$" from top edge seamline.

$1/4$" seam allowance

$4\frac{1}{4}$"

Top edge

$1/4$" seam allowance

CENTER FRONT PANEL

Leather: cut 1

Center front

$9\frac{1}{8}$"

Center back matchpoint on center back panel only

Side of bag matchpoints on side front panels only

Cut-up-to line = green at $1/2$" from side cut edge

$4\frac{1}{8}$"

$3/8$" Seam allowance

Side of bag matchpoint

$1/4$" seam allowance

Cut up to line at $1/2$" from cut edge.

$3/8$" seam allowance

Base matchpoint

$5\frac{1}{8}$"

Note on weaving cuts: On center front panel and two side back wedge panels, the cuts begin $1/4$" down from top edge seamline.

Place-metal-edge line = red at $^{11}/_{16}$" from side cut edge
cut up to line = green at $1/2$" from side cut edge